W9-AVE-686

"A Remnant . . ."

Statement of Purpose

The Holocaust spread across the face of Europe almost fifty years ago. The brutality then unleashed is still nearly beyond comprehension. Millions of innocents, men, women and children, were consumed by its flames.

The goal of Holocaust Publications, a non-profit organization founded by survivors, is to publish and disseminate works on the Holocaust. These will include survivors' accounts, testimonies and memoirs, historical and regional analyses, anthologies, archival and source documents and other relevant materials that will help shed light on this cataclysmic era.

These books and studies will be made available to the general public, scholars, researchers, historians, teachers and students. They will be used in Holocaust Resource Centers, libraries and schools, synagogues and churches. They will help foster an increased awareness of the Holocaust and its implications. They will help *to preserve the memory* for posterity and to enable this awesome time to be better understood and comprehended.

Holocaust Library
216 West 18th Street
New York, NY 10011

"A Remnant..."

by
Jacob Barosin

HOLOCAUST LIBRARY
New York

DS
135
F83
B37
1988

Copyright © 1988 by Jacob Barosin

Library of Congress Catalogue Card Number 88-80085

ISBN: 0-89604-093-5 (Cloth)
0-89604-129-8 (Paper)

Original Cover Art by Jacob Barosin
Cover Design by The Appelbaum Company

Printed in the United States of America

ROBERT MANNING
STROZIER LIBRARY

JUN 8 1990

Tallahassee, Florida

Library of Congress Cataloging-in-Publication Data

Barosin, Jacob.
   "A remnant --"

   1. Jews--France--Persecutions.   2. Holocaust,
Jewish (1939-1945)--France--Personal narratives.
3. Barosin, Jacob.   4. France--Ethnic relations.
I. Title.
DS135.F83B37   1988   940.53'15'03924044   88-8008
ISBN 0-89604-129-8 (pbk.)

"Yet a remnant of them will return . . ."

— Isaiah, 10:22

This book is dedicated to the memory of Sonia

Preface

IN THESE PAGES is told the true story, from 1940 to 1944, of a young Jewish couple in France, arrested, imprisoned and rearrested, in and out of concentration camps, in one hiding place and then another, confined to a small room for months, constantly on the run from the Gestapo and the police authorities that sought to add them to the martyrs of the Holocaust.

I tell my story and that of my wife, of those years not as a skilled writer but as a witness who has lived and gone through that terrible time in Europe and who feels strongly that a survivor's account is essential in understanding this critical period in occupied Europe. These years in France come to life: hundreds of thousands were delivered by Vichy to the Germans; but when also many, many thousands of us were saved by brave and decent French people. The latter reacted courageously to this greatest catastrophe in their nation's history and honored French Civilization and humanitarianism. On the other, hand a presumed cultured nation had collapsed under the onslaught of barbarism.

You will meet some people who responded to the challenge of Evil, risking their own lives for us. You will read about human decency at work and plain goodness of heart and mind that spoke louder at times than the abject and subhuman murder machinery that the Germans had built.

This young persecuted couple had to cope psychologically, ethically and materially with completely unforeseen, dangerous and often unbelievable conditions. It may appear to some as passive resistance, inglorious and unsung; but whatever we did in order to survive and to keep two individuals of our people alive, was a day and night battle we fought in our own way. No partisan, no maquis (Resistance) guns reached our hands, but in constant struggle, with tension and often through quick thinking decisions, we had to have courage and faith, prudence and perseverance.

Some cruel and ignorant people chose to blame us for not having fought more glamorously and heroically. We waged a five year war for life and human dignity on our deadly enemy. We stayed alive, we survived, that is to say: we won.

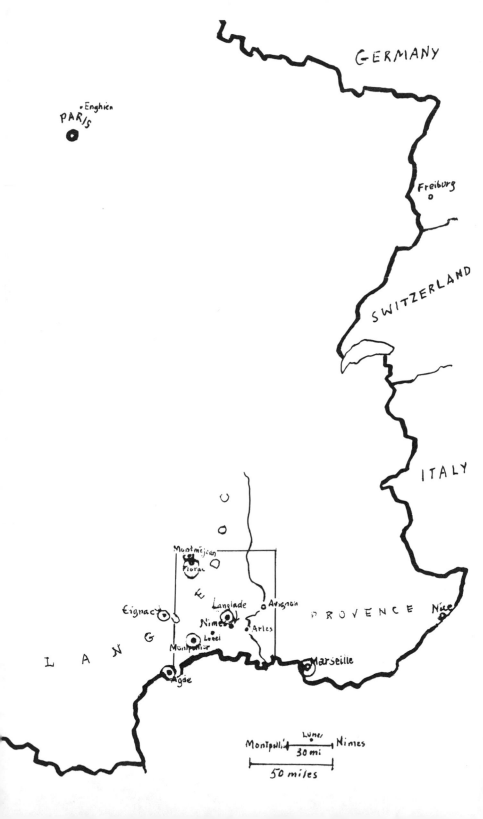

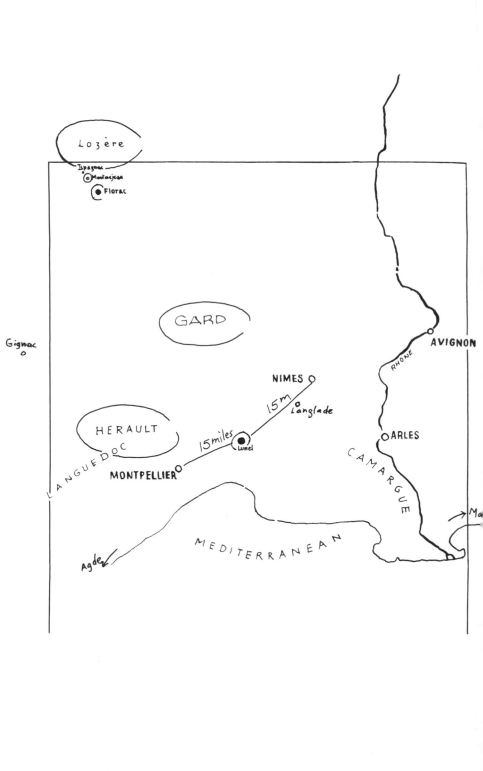

1

BEWILDERED AND FRIGHTENED we stood there, Sonia and I, at the corner of Berlin's Kurfurstendamm watching those goose stepping, noisily singing, torch carrying and flag-swinging storm-troopers who by the thousands had come out to celebrate Hitler's seizure of power on this 30th day of January 1933.

The crowds on the sidewalks were delirious, screaming, singing, holding up little swastika flags. There was a ground-swell of German irrationality, this massive and instinctive *Furor Teutonicus* that Tacitus writes about, this trance created by the heavy marching and deadly music.

The ancient German tale of the Pied Piper, the rat exterminator of Hameln, came to my mind who, centuries ago, had led the children of that town to the river where they all drowned. The tune which the unrewarded and angry pipe-player produced was so alluring that all the kids marched singing behind him to their death. And here, this fateful night, hundreds of thousands of Berliners went overboard in their frenzy, their enthusiasm and their blind obedience to a leader that had promised to free them from all their *ills*, the central cause of which—naturally—were the Jews.

We have a sixth sense, we Jews, developed in thousands of years of catastrophes, assassinations, persecutions, pogroms, expulsions and insults: the sense of smelling danger while others are still dancing on the volcano. Like a seismograph we register the eruption still miles and years away, because we are the first to suffer the impact. We looked at each other, my wife and I, and we knew that we had to leave this traditionally anti-Semitic country and its flood of hate, a country which anyway was not ours and which hit us in the face with its slogan *Germany Awake, Juda Perish* or its obscene song: *When Jew blood drips from our knives, things will be so much better.*

Six months later Sonia and I found ourselves in a small hotel room in Paris, hoping that we could survive our four-week visa in this country of Liberty, Equality and Fraternity. We were right. We stayed on for fifteen years. We were aware of the fact that hundreds and thousands of Central and East European refugees were pressing towards the French frontier and that the French Authorities had a duty to protect the jobs of French workers. As we learned later, no other country had accepted as many refugees as France had done during the economically and politically difficult years preceding World War II. However we were ill prepared for the harsh winds of Prefecture harassment of *Undesirables* (that is penniless aliens) who—as a rule—were denied the right to work. But what does administrative and judicial legality mean to those who fight for their lives. In Germany we were persecuted as Jews and we were promised that our blood would drip from their knives. Here in France we were refused working papers.

Being in our early twenties, we were both poorly prepared to cope with the anxieties and tensions that came from working illegally, with one foot in prison or on the expulsion train back to dark Germany. A good foreigner was the one who abides by the law and starves. We did not abide by the laws of those days, but we did not starve.

Though a Russian citizen by birth, I had been reared in Germany and had completed my education with a Ph.D. in Art History from Freiburg University shortly before 1933, while it was still possible for an ambitious young Jew to graduate from a German University. Before switching to University and scientific research, I had studied a few years at the prestigious Staats-Schulen for Free and Applied Art at the Steinplatz in Berlin.

As a very young girl Sonia had studied the violin in her hometown Odessa (Russia); then after fleeing with her parents the Russian Revolution, she had found employment in an orchestra in Rumania, and ended up at the Berlin University and the Stern Conservatory to complete her studies. Here we met at a piano, where I accompanied her, and later we got married.

We both were Russian Jews, foreigners in Germany. We had

grown up in homes where our holidays were celebrated with gusto, where the pride in our ancient civilization had been nurtured and developed in our hearts. My father especially was enthusiastic not only about the 3000 year old literature of the Hebrew people, but about its unequalled contribution to Civilization in every field of human endeavor. And though there was an unavoidable generation gap between my father and his teenage son, in this respect our views were always identical. To this day, I thank my father for his insights and his influence.

Sonia and I had chosen the right professions as far as our talents, inclinations and intellectual drives were concerned, but certainly the wrong ones when it came to making a living and to putting food into our stomachs. So it did not take long to find out that our careers in Art History, in painting and music had come to an abrupt end before they even had a chance to start; we understood that we had to make a living in our new host country with anything that came up. Besides we had to face and to fight the less than friendly attitude of the French Administration that considered us greedy bread snatchers from the mouths of French citizens. I shall never forget the witty remark of a civil servant at the Prefecture who extended the validity of my identity paper.

"You have a Ph.D. — In which discipline?"

"Philosophy, Histoire de l'Art" (Art History).

"Things do change, don't they; now it becomes l'histoire du lard" (the story of finding lard).

There were however two elements that gave us the strength to pull through those difficult years after our arrival in Paris. The young love and respect we had for each other was one asset. The other was an age old experience in our Jewish blood to face and to conquer all obstacles that were accumulated on our road to survival. My father and my mother with their two small children had left Russia shortly before World War I, and my father — starting at zero — had climbed the ladder as a foreign plywood importer to a comfortable middle class status in Berlin. Sonia's father, born in Kishinev (Bessarabia) had brought as a young man to Odessa his painful poverty and an irresistible will to succeed financially. He achieved his goal in a remarkable way in the wholesale lumber business.

I knew that the times and the situation had completely changed for us, coming from Central Europe to France, a country that had only suspicion and contempt for everything that moved in from beyond the Rhine. If our fathers could hope to amass a little fortune in the first twenty years of this century in Europe, I knew that during the thirties we would need in France all our wits to just survive, and all our cleverness and agility when violating the Law that denied us working papers.

I put my Art historical research and my brushes away for a while and became a salesman for printing matters. I found two Russian Jews who had installed printing shops in Paris years ago, when this had still been feasible for foreigners, and they gave me a good commission on the orders I brought in. Sonia who had always been very good with her hands when it came to sewing, embroidering, knitting etc. found some ladies for whom she sewed dresses. By 1935 we were out of the woods and arranged things in such a way that we could not be caught by the Police.

How can this be done? First I matriculated as a student at the Sorbonne. Second I took out a license as a businessman (Registre du Commerce). Business and investment were encouraged, because they might bring in taxes, spending money and employment for French people. So I took out a business license as an advertisement agency, though I had never been a businessman, nor did I have any money to invest. A year later they did not give you that license so easily.

Now besides the elementary Stomach Law which says, "Feed your wife and yourself," there was the Right of Residence Law in France with a lot of restrictions and small print that haunted us for a long time. During the first eighteen months we had to get a three month permit to stay on, renewable each time for three more months. You lost your sleep almost automatically eight or ten days before you had to drag yourself to the Prefecture to have your receipt extended. After that period of a year and a half we got a foreigner's identity card for a whole year's right to stay on French soil. Nobody who has ever held this treasure for the first time in his fingers knows what the feeling of *security* for twelve good months means. You are not in France, you are in heaven.

In 1934 we had rented a four room apartment on the 9th floor under the roof at 94, Rue St. Lazare, a large business street that passes the St. Lazare Railroad Station. It was not an apartment but an office building, and nobody but the two of us and the Super lived there. After 5 or 6 PM an impenetrable silence fell on this big house, but we got used to it. From our little balcony we had a splendid view over this beautiful city in all directions: Trinité, Opera, Eiffel Tower, Sacré Coeur on its Montmartre and many more which I sketched and painted often. Some days the dark clouds dramatically chase each other, some days the sun bathes the old roofs and houses in pastel colors. At times the sky is clothed in a pinkish gray, a kind of Degas-gray; or it just rains as everywhere, and that is the end for a painter.

People were not used to the kind of luxury, in those days, that today we believe to be indispensable. There was no bathroom in the house. If you really wanted and felt that you needed a bath, there was a Public Bath half a mile away. A tiny W.C. in the hallway served the employees of four offices on the floor and us. The kitchen was no real kitchen, but a portable two burner plate next to a small water sink, 18 inches wide, ancient and leaking. There we did our cooking, washing, laundry, shaving, what have you. But I suppose happiness and comfort are two different things. We were young, we were healthy, we were out of Germany, we had a one-year residence permit in Paris, we were still in love after a few years of marriage; material discomfort was unable to interfere with our happiness. Somerset Maugham once said: "If you have only green beans for dinner, but you eat them under a roof in Paris, count yourself lucky." This is how we felt. Sonia and I had married cousins in Paris and a few friends, so our social life began to organize. We started to integrate into the life of this great, civilized, charming and beautiful city. It had become "Home".

I am not going to tell the story of the ups and downs of our almost seven years before the War in Paris. Of course we would have loved to go on forever peacefully in our new surroundings. But fate and History had other plans.

World War II had broken out in Europe the first day of September 1939, but for eight long months *all was quiet on the western front,* that is to say on the French border. These eight months we called *La drôle de guerre,* the funny war, because nothing seemed to happen, and a disquieting calm, a frightful expectation of terrible things to come had descended upon us.

I find in my short diary of those days under May 11, 1940 the following entry:

"Yesterday, May, 10, the funny war came to an end and the shooting war began near France with a big bang. The Germans seem to have invaded Holland—which they have not done in World War I—and everybody knows that the resistance of the brave Dutch people can only be symbolic. Next will be the Belgians to taste their aggression. Everybody here in Paris is upset and worried. Though big posters tell us in big words: *We will win because we are the stronger ones,* many people have great apprehensions as to the events of the next few days and weeks; there is a cloud of extreme pessimism, even of despair in the air. Will the Maginot Line hold? The Germans have more planes than the French and British can muster together. Until yesterday we lived like in a dream; the war was not real. Czechoslavakia had fallen, Poland had fallen, in Norway and in Finland there had been fighting, but they are so far from France. With wishful thinking and a little prayer maybe we could go on like this in a kind of twilight zone between the shooting war somewhere else and the drôle de guerre in France. Of course we knew it could not last, but we wished so much to be left alone that we almost had thought it could be done. Now this atrocious war which had not been real for us, became real yesterday, the 10th of May. We had stocked some food; Sonia says we would need some more. She may be right as women mostly are when it comes to practical things; we will buy whatever we can find. Who knows how many months we will be cut off from regular food supply. There may be a siege of Paris . . ."

The air was full of rumors. From the St. Lazare Station two blocks from our apartment, trainloads of soldiers were leaving. We would have to live from day to day, since I might be called up soon. I had enlisted as a volunteer, a year ago, to serve in the French Army and to do my duty toward this good country that had given us hospitality when, in 1933, we had fled Germany. I was a stateless person and as far as I could remember, I had always been stateless. To be sure, it is not much of a nationality, it is no nationality at all. Sonia fleeing as a very young girl with her parents during the early 1920s from communism in Russia, first to Bessarabia and then to Bukowina (Rumania), had acquired for some very tangible reasons the Rumanian nationality. But she had lost it when, in Berlin, she married me, a stateless student. I have often been asked how does a man lose his nationality and become stateless? I will tell this story later, because at this point so many things happened every hour.

Boris, Sonia's cousin (also from Odessa) called: he wanted us to come over to see them. He, Paulette and their little girl lived in Boulogne s/Seine, half an hour by subway from St. Lazare. Boris and I had become good friends. He was a fine pianist, but piano playing did not fill the stomach. There in Paris he had a little shop, selling fruit and vegetables, a far cry from Bach and Chopin. Boris told me that for the time being he would stay on with his family, but we all should consider sending our wives away, if possible to Southern France. Who had the money for that? I had just brought Sonia back from Quimiac, a little village in Normandy, where she had spent the first six months of the war with some Russian women. War is a hazardous thing. You have to be lucky. If you do not believe in your luck, no place will give you safety. I wondered when they would call me for military duty. I had undergone the medical test by the Military Authorities and was found apt and fit for military service. What would become of Sonia when I would have to leave her? Boris and Paulette promised that they would take care of her if need be. They were far from being rich; however their kind offer reassured me. Wherever they would go—if they had to flee Paris—they would take Sonia with them. My dear wife worried so much and tried to hide it from me. But since she did not play her violin any more—which she had done every day—I knew how she really felt. She had not played for over a week; who could anyway under the circumstances.

A few days later Belgium was overrun. King Leopold did not flee like the Dutch Queen had done; he found that he could live with them. Business in Paris came to a halt. There were no new commissions or orders for printing or advertisement drawings. Everything had stopped. Everybody took a deep breath as before going underwater for a while. I was running around talking to customers, cashing some as yet unpaid bills and checks. Everybody was nervous and edgy. People who could do so were leaving Paris. The trains and the roads were full.

Here we were, sitting on the volcano that had begun to erupt. The newspapers tried to calm the people, but on the Radio here and there a word, a sentence, revealed the terrible uneasiness. Rumors of a complete breakdown swirled around. There are always people who are quick to preach defeatism; pessimists for whom the glass will always be half empty. But how good were the French military defenses really? At this point this was the only thing that counted, not the posters all around town that promised us victory.

I went to the American Consulate near the Place de la Concorde to see whether my application for a visa, submitted many months ago, could be acted upon or the procedure somehow accelerated. But since I did not as yet have the necessary affidavit from an American citizen, the whole thing seemed more than problematic. Anyway the official, though quite polite, did not give me much hope, but told me to come back next week for more information. What else is there to do but to sit and to wait, with the rest of France.

2

So MANY THINGS happened to us during the next twelve days that I would not know where to begin. The 18th of May (1940) started out as every other day: breakfast, taking the elevator down to see if there was any mail at the super's office, buying bread and the newspaper. Then I started writing an overdue letter.

"Maybe tonight we go to see a movie?" Sonia said.

"What a splendid idea; just to get our minds off our problems. What would you like to see?"

"I will look up the movie program in the newspaper".

She continued reading the paper, and I went on writing. Suddenly the bell rang. We looked at each other. Who in the world could that be at 11:30 in the morning? We did not expect anybody. I got up and opened the door. There were two tall men who sized me up. One showed me a kind of identity card and put it away so fast that I could not read it, but I heard him say: *Préfecture de Police.* He asked my name and entered the room; the other one left. Sonia came out into the hall.

"Are you Mrs. Barosin?"

"Yes, I am."

"You will both have to follow me to the Precinct".

"For what reason?" I venture.

"Oh, I don't know. I just have to bring you over there. I would advise you to take, each one, a suitcase with some underwear and pullovers. The nights are still cool".

"Nights? So we would not go home today?" I was upset.

"I am afraid not".

"Could we make a few telephone calls to friends?"

"One call is allowed." He became annoyed.

"So we are arrested?"

"You will be given all the information at the Precinct, Mister". "Mister" meant: dont ask any more stupid questions and hurry up. Sonia and I went into the bedroom, divided the money we had between us, hid it in small bags on our chests and started packing our suitcases. We had hardly time to look at each other. The door to the other room had to be open. We called Boris to tell him that we were about to be arrested and to leave the apartment, that he should inform his brother Jacques and our other friends, and that we would call him or write to him as soon as possible so he should know our whereabouts. In his voice I noticed that he was more nervous than we were.

When we left the apartment and locked the door, the policeman sealed the lock. That did not look good at all. With French politeness he took Sonia's suitcase and carried it down to his car. A thought flashed through my mind: I will not be able any more to visit the American Consulate . . .

Thinking now about the Buffalo Stadium episode, where I was interned with thousands of mostly German speaking refugees, the events of the 18th of May and the following days took on a nightmare like, unreal flavor.

Once at the Precinct of the 9th Arrondissement (Paris is divided into 20 Arrondissements, or sectors) our guard delivered us to the policeman on duty, had a slip signed and left. We sat down on a bench, the suitcases before our knees, barriers between us and the outside world which became increasingly hostile. How long were we there on this bench? Twenty minutes, half an hour? I do not know. There are hours and days which flow by like an endless little brook, monotonously, slowly, in a vague sameness. But there are times in life when seconds and minutes are of the utmost importance, filled with drama and action, and when one has to make the best he can to retain the essence of those minutes. We had the clear feeling, Sonia and I, that we would soon be separated; we knew that we would not see each other for a long time—maybe never.

"There must be an error," I whispered to Sonia, trying to calm her.

"The Prefecture did not arrest us at the outbreak of the War in

September 1939, when they arrested all German and Austrian Jews and Non-Jews. We were not molested because we are stateless as is Boris, i.e. of Russian origin. Furthermore, the Prefecture that had us arrested now did not know of my military status, namely that I had signed up for military duty. It does not make sense that they would arrest a future French soldier. This whole misunderstanding will be cleared up as soon as I show them my papers and my signing up for the War. We should be home shortly."

Sonia was not completely convinced. But she wanted so much to believe what I said that at the word *home* she gave me a fine smile. I went on talking to her, trying to find all kind of reasons why this arrest had to be an error. Then I made sure that she had all the addresses and telephone numbers of our friends and cousins. Suddenly the sirens began to wail. A bombing attack on Paris? Everybody became nervous in the Precinct. The police officer who was in charge of us asked us to follow him quickly into the shelter in the basement. And there we sat, two quiet arrested foreigners together with the agitated French policemen, facing somehow the same danger of being bombed out together by the same enemy. I offered them cigarettes; we smoked and made small talk. Half an hour later, the end of the alert was sounded. After the end of the emergency (there had been no air attack) everything came back to normal: we went back upstairs with our suitcases and again we became distrusted, arrested foreigners for these French policemen.

"Mr. and Mrs. Barosin?"

"Yes." We got up and approached his desk.

"You will be sent to two stadiums here in Paris.

Madame, you will go to the Vélodrome d'Hiver, and you, Monsieur, to the Buffalo Stade. There your papers will be examined, and if they are in order, you will be released in a few days. Otherwise you will be sent to reception centers (what an elegant euphemism for a Concentration Camp) to await further developments. You will leave here as soon as the special bus is ready".

"But sir," I replied, "I enlisted in the French Army even before the War broke out to do my duty." I nervously unfolded the precious piece of paper before his nose, stating that I had enlisted and passed the examination by a Military Council.

"I am now expecting a call any day to be inducted," I went on. "Under those circumstances, why do you arrest my wife and me?

You did not arrest us at the beginning of the War, when all those who came from Central Europe . . ."

"Monsieur," he interrupted me, "I have my orders here from the Préfecture. You will explain your case and your papers at the Buffalo Stade, and I am certain that they will decide in your favor. There is no point in insisting here".

Another policeman whispered something in his ear.

"As a matter of fact," our man went on, "the special bus just arrived; follow me".

We were not a little surprised to see that it was not a bus, but a prisoner van, a "Salad Basket" (panier à salade) as it is called in France in which prisoners were transfered from one prison to another; and we were not in such good company, to be sure.

We were driven down the Champs Elysees, and the people who had their cups of coffee or their early evening aperitif in those numerous open bistros (as we had had sometimes before) looked at our prisoner van and almost reproachfully into our faces. I realized suddenly that some catastrophe was coming down on our heads and that we would need all our strength to go through the storm that was gathering. We did not talk, Sonia and I. I put my arm around her shoulder and pressed her against me.

The van first went to the Vélodrome d'Hiver. I embraced and kissed my wife. She was pale when she turned around at the gate before being taken away by a policeman. I never had felt the real meaning of loneliness and helplessness as at this moment. We were in the hands of others who decided where we would go and what would happen to us. We were no longer our own masters.

I was brought to the Buffalo Stadium, to one of those long and narrow benches on which hundreds of thousands of fans had followed, enthusiastically, in better days, soccer and other sporting events. There were about two thousand foreigners who were waiting to see what the Camp Administration would do with them. I could not get over the fact that something had happened that had taken my fate out of my hands, something that had an unreal dimension, as if you lose foot on top of an ice-covered hill and are gliding, falling down an endless slope, not knowing if and when you will again be on your feet.

Eventually my identity was entered into some files; my protests were not even listened to. I was given a blanket and told to find a place for the night somewhere on or between the benches.

Those who had been there before me and who now became my bench-neighbors, told me that the first thing to look for was a bowl or a pot or a can, into which some soup would soon be poured. Someone took me to a huge heap of garbage where he found an empty can that did not look very clean; we went to the pump and cleaned it as well as we could. Because there were so many newcomers that day, the chickpea soup—which I will never forget —and a piece of stale bread were distributed at 8 PM. We were hungry and ate it.

Rumors were making the round: the French front had been broken or bypassed on many points by hundreds of German Panzers, the French army was in full retreat, and the High Command was trying to find a line to re-establish the French resistance. The question now arose: will it be North of Paris or somewhere in the center of France. If the German offensive was faster than the French defense could be reorganized, we here in Buffalo Stadium would all become prisoners of the Nazis. My thoughts were racing: for us there is no escape possible. Would we be evacuated to some other place? The roads and railroads were clogged with refugees; the military reinforcements could not pass on the roads because of the civilians fleeing South in their cars, horsedrawn wagons and on their bicycles. And the Germans kept bombing and strafing the roads. There were thousands of casualties and not enough hospitals, doctors and nurses. *C'est la pagaille*. This is complete chaos. But don't tell anybody; people can be shot for defeatism.

The first day I was in a daze. But humans are strange animals; there were those who just played cards and told jokes. They came from all walks of life: merchants, artisans, ex-professors, ex-civil servants, shopkeepers, students and others. They were mostly German and Austrian Jews, some came from Poland and Russia. Some of the German Jews, of course hostile to the German government, resented their arrest by the French authorities and were rather indifferent to the news of German military advances. I thought only: keep away from them; some were dangerous in their stupidity—or were there already spies among us? We had in Buffalo some non-Jews, some incorrigible Communists whose long political tirades one did not really have to listen to. They had recently become buddy-buddy with the Nazis (after the Ribbentrop-Molotov Pact). Of course the French arrested them.

I was all this time without news from Sonia.

Then I asked for and received permission to leave the Camp for three hours. There was no point in going to our sealed apartment at Rue St. Lazare. I called Jacques, Boris's brother and Sonia's other cousin. He was not in, but Jeanne, his wife, told me that she had received a letter from Sonia (one could write from inside the Camp, but not receive letters there) telling her that on the 25th of May the Vélodrome d'Hiver would be emptied and that the women and children would all be sent to the huge Camp of Gurs in the Pyrenees, near the Spanish border. She asked Jeanne to let me know, if she could. She asked her to save her violin from our apartment, if it was at all possible. Jeanne promised me to do it, even if she had to break the seals. I was very moved by her determination. I thanked her, knowing what the violin meant to Sonia who had saved it on her flight from Russia, almost as her only treasured possession. Then I called Boris, who lived much closer to Buffalo Stade, and he came right away to see me. We met in a little coffee shop not far from there.

We embraced and tried to smile, and then we unpacked. First I told him in detail what had happened, arrest and all. Naturally, I wanted to know how the military situation in France was shaping up. Unless a miracle occurs, he said, and miracles are very rare, Paris would fall into the enemy's hands sooner rather than later. According to the latest bulletins, the High Command admitted that the Germans were about 120 miles from Paris. There was no real and organized defense or resistance any more. At this point Boris and Paulette did not know what they were going to do. His mother-in-law had friends in Brittany; maybe they could go there, but they had too little money. They probably would just have to stay in Paris, where they could make a living in their shop. We talked for over an hour and said good-bye, knowing that we would not meet for a long time.

The War came to each of us; every life was in danger. In this respect a 20th century war makes no difference between soldier and civilian.

I was back at the stadium in time. My neighbors and some new friends asked me what was going on in the outside world. I toned down the fearful interpretations of Boris. I did not want to appear to be a rumor monger and a pessimist. Besides you never know who was listening in. In my new environment one had to be very circumspect and prudent, especially a young man like me who had always indulged in the luxury of saying what he thought and what he meant to say.

I did some sketching of inmates or internees or prisoners, call them as you wish.

The pace of events was now ·accelerating quickly. In the beginning of June I found myself in Southern France, in a small village called Langlade located 13 km SW of Nîmes. What the policeman in the Paris Precinct had told me was true: In the Buffalo Stade we were grouped according to age and loyalty to France (voluntary enlistment). On June 2 about two hundred of us, mostly younger men, were saved from the German takeover. We were sent by train to Nîmes, where we arrived very early in the morning of the 3rd. The news about the War was terrifying. Sporadic fighting was still going on but with a foregone conclusion: France was defeated. The Army had been incapable of stopping the German offensive. Paris had fallen and the Germans had paraded through the Arch of Triumph along the Champs Elysees on June 14th.

Things were unbelievable and bewildering. Everybody was feeling in his personal life the shocks and tremors of the world moving quickly, of historic events that could change the face of mankind. The government of France fled to Bordeaux. There was little talk now about establishing a new front on French soil; on the contrary: armistice talks and peace feelers were being rumored. Mussolini took advantage of the situation to declare war on France and Britain. Was this the end of the war, the end of France as a power to be reckoned with, we asked.

I could finally write a letter to Sonia and give her my address, knowing that she was in the Camp of Gurs and that mail got through to her.

Marshal Pétain had taken over the government from Paul Reynaud. At 84 years of age, the beloved hero of World War I, instead of saving France, became its gravedigger in World War II. On June 16, 1940, Pétain officially asked the Germans to state their terms for an armistice. Would he now hand us over to the Germans? Rumors were rampant in Langlade. When we were finally sick and tired of them, we went for a walk in the surroundings of this pleasant little Languedoc village, embedded in hills filled with vineyards. This is wine country, and as far as the eye can see there is the ancient wine culture of Southern France.

Arriving from Paris fifteen days earlier, on the 3rd of June, we were taken to the Artillery Depot in Nîmes and from there by truck to the Langlade Cantonment, where we were given our "prestataire" uniforms, a brown beret, a working suit, a brown cape and two blankets. A Prestataire is a military worker, an auxiliary to the armed soldier; we were not given arms. Had the War not come to an unexpected end, we probably would have had to dig trenches, to do heavy and at times dangerous work. The cantonment was a big old cow or horse barn with strawbags (our beds) on the floor, leaving enough space in between for our meager belongings. The cows and horses were gone, but the fleas and bedbugs had stayed and multiplied by the millions which made it very difficult to fall asleep. After a fight of many hours with those ferocious little animals you became so exhausted that you just gave up.

There was not much to do in Langlade in those days, only to sit around, to wait, to get bored, almost like in Buffalo. The Commanding Officer and the sergeants tried to keep us busy as much as they could. Once we were ordered to march all day long, passing through Clarensac, Calvisson, old medieval villages. We made about twenty miles altogether. It did our rusty bones some good and it took our minds off our worries. But the sergeants were so tired out that they needed some rest and never tried again. Of course France, Europe, world events were on our minds; they ran like a base counter, or lower tenor, through our feelings and our thinking. However, it is surprising to what extent the preoccupation with our personal situation, our own lives and future, took precedence over political and military occurrences that have changed the fate of entire nations.

3

FOR JEWS, GERMANY'S victory was a catastrophe of unimaginable dimensions, and for each of us—we knew—there could be a tragedy in store that we were as yet unable to fathom. Even though we were certain that the events of the next few years must bring a crushing defeat of Germany—as World War I did—we were not so sure that the German future debacle would come in time to save us Jews in Europe from annihilation. When it comes to anti-Semitic hatred, the Germans would find many brothers-in-arms in many quarters.

There were two hundred men in our prestataire group, from 23 to 45 years of age, who increased greatly the population of this village of 150 souls. A kind of little restaurant with a garden, where rustic tables and chairs invited the newcomers, was always full of gesticulating men who threw their more or less intelligent opinions at each other. Most of them were still without news from their wives and children, except one who expected his wife to arrive in Langlade from the Camp of Gurs. We married men were very recently given the permission to send a certificate of our *presence at the prestataire group 312* in Langlade to our wives in Gurs, a certificate which would cause their immediate release and entitle them to a safe-conduct pass to wherever they wanted to go. I sent one registered to Sonia, so she should be freed soon and come to Langlade.

In the meantime, unable to sleep in that cantonment, I rented with three other prestataires, Weingarten, Schauder and Reich an old house from Madame Vieilledent (Old-tooth) who kept a village grocery store in Upper Langlade. The house had two rooms and a windowless kitchen with a huge fireplace, located in one of those old, narrow medieval streets with very uneven pavement. The monthly rent of fr. 40 (about three dollars) was more than reasonable. We put double strawbags—the cleanest we could find—into the two upper rooms, found somewhere an old green table still standing on its four shaky legs, and two benches. This was home now. No electricity, but Mrs. Vieilledent sold us a lot of candles. There was no toilet whatsoever. This was an urgent problem to be solved. The water pump was—conveniently—at the corner of the street. Where would I put up Sonia if and when she came? There was of course no hotel in little Langlade. But let her first be freed and come, then we will think of something.

A few days later I had a letter from Sonia saying that thanks to my certificate she would be liberated from the camp of Gurs around the 25th of June and would travel to Langlade the next day. As a matter of fact, a few refugee women had already appeared in our village which made it almost impossible to find some sleeping place for a night or two. Maybe I could find a room in a neighboring village. Mrs. Vieilledent sold me under the table a sausage, a chocolate bar and a few eggs for the great occasion, but I had to promise to tell nobody.

From my Diary again: "New rumors abound in Langlade. Since the war is practically over—the fighting lasted 37 days—prestataire groups will be dissolved, and we will be distributed among 'real' Concentration Camps. Where? When? Mystery. Or we may be handed over to the Germans who will do with us as they please. Many among us had been German citizens before; they too had signed up before the War to fight against the Germans. All of us might just be shot. Nobody would ever know about it. Another terrible thing that could happen was that they would take us out of France and ship us back to Germany. An armistice is being signed by Pétain. What transpires is that there will be a free zone (free from German Military, certainly not from Gestapo); about 2/5 of France, the Southern part, where we are.

"Pétain put two men in power: Pierre Laval, his Vice-President and Raphael Aribert from the Action Francaise (arch-reactionary and anti-Semitic). We know what that means for us. A kind of government will be established in the Free Zone in Vichy. All these and many more things are worrying us a great deal. But for the time being there is joy in my heart: Sonia may come home tomorrow or after tomorrow . . ."

And then she arrived in Langlade, on the 26th of June, in the morning. We had a tearful reunion; in the afternoon we went looking for a room. No chance. The rooms we saw were not better than my room. So Weingarten, my roommate, left, and we left our problem for tomorrow. Anyway this room was not good enough for a non-soldier and I would not ask my wife to stay there for any length of time. But frightful and hectic events unrolled quickly.

The next morning, June 27, we had an unexpected guest: One of the three policemen of Langlade paid us a visit and let us know that he had come to arrest Sonia, because as a foreigner she had to produce a legalized permit to stay in the Department of Gard, where Langlade is located, and she had none. She would be put into a concentration camp. Hearing this, Sonia broke down, because by now she knew what a concentration camp was. I had my hands full to negotiate with the Policeman and to plead for a little time, a day or two, so we could get the necessary paper in the Préfecture at Nîmes; on the other hand I had to calm and to encourage Sonia who was sitting there and crying quietly. The policeman was no monster. He said that though he had orders to arrest Mrs. Barosin, he could—instead of today—do it tomorrow, and he left. After he was out of the house, I said to Sonia:

"You will not stay here. Let me see your safe-conduct paper from Gurs to Langlade".

It was a printed form of a *Sauf-Conduit* and in black ink her name was written in, with the words *from Gurs to Langlade (Gard).*

"You will not stay in Langlade; this is obviously not a place for you. And you will not go to another Concentration Camp either. What about going to the Riviera where we have such good friends who would help, and where we have spent the most beautiful vacations. You go to Nice and wait there for me when I will be discharged."

"Your imagination runs off with you," she replied. "Where do I get a safe-conduct to Nice? Certainly not in Langlade where they are ready to arrest me tomorrow to put me into a Camp."

"Let me worry about that. I will get you a safe-conduct to Nice right away. Wait for me here. I'll be back in ten minutes, but don't cry. Give me your paper."

I rushed off to the Post Office where in an old ink well they had the most beautiful black ink, matching the color of the ink on the paper. The employee at the window, not knowing what I needed it for, lent me his pen, and I added after the words *Langlade (Gard)* the four words: *et Nice, Alpes Maritimes* in a handwriting which was unmistakably the same as the other one; I had done some exercising on a piece of paper before.

I did not walk home; I ran.

"Put your things together and prepare your suitcase. There seems to be a train from Nîmes to Nice around 4 PM. Let me ask Mrs. Sachs who has a car to bring you from here to Nîmes."

"But I don't have a safe-conduct and I won't go on a train without one."

"Here is your brand-new safe-conduct." Sonia's face lit up and she kissed me.

Mrs. Sachs, the wife of a man with whom I had become friendly, did not need a lot of explanations, and she did not accept any money from me. In fifteen minutes she would be at the Railroad Station. I kissed my wife good-bye. An hour later Mrs. Sachs was back from Nîmes where she had waited until Sonia was on the train to Nice.

When, the next morning, the policeman came for Sonia, I gave him the good news:

"My wife had to leave urgently, an aunt fell sick."

He smiled, relieved that he did not have to arrest such a nice girl and said:

"I think you did the right thing under those circumstances."

We shook hands. Stepping out, he turned around: "Good luck for your aunt," and we had a good laugh.

Soon thereafter a letter from Sonia reassured me.

The first night in Nice she spent in a hotel, but the next morning she went looking for a room and she rented one in Cimiez-Nice, not far from the ruins of the Roman Arena. Our good friends knew a police officer who probably would give her a residence paper which would allow her to stay in Nice. I thought about these turbulent last days and I discovered that even when circumstances are rudely against you, there is often a small chance—at times imperceptibly small—for your personal intervention and for your taking the sting out of the flesh. Without her brand-new *safe-conduct* Sonia would have been in a concentration camp by now. Instead of that she could at present swim in the Mediterranean and enjoy the Nice beach which, unfortunately, is not much of a beach, but a stretch of pebbles.

The most frightening aspect of the kind of life during those months was that we did not know what would happen to us the next week, even the next day. Mixed up with those unusual worries were the rather usual money problems of a young stateless emigree in Europe in 1940. Naturally, my living expenses in Langlade were minimal, but we had only a few thousand francs left. For Nice that was not much.

4

AFTER A FEW relaxed days I began to worry again and I felt—as far as worrying is concerned—I was in business for a long time. There was no lack of rumors. It became obvious that since the end of the war prestataires were a useless commodity and that the Army would get rid of us. Probably we would become part of a concentration camp full of dispensable foreigners, administered by the Labor or Interior Ministry. I only prayed that we should remain in French hands and not be *loaned* to the Germans.

I knew I had to make an effort to think of something to get out of this lamentable Langlade situation. Not only was our future ominous, but the mere fact of being surrounded by frightened, often desperate people, many of whom dreaded the Germans and hated the French, created an ambiguous atmosphere for a man who was always full of admiration for the French civilization and who liked the French people. Except for a few cultured men who had more understanding than the crowd, I was fast becoming an outsider. After all I was not one of the German Jews who had assimilated too lovingly to Germanism, but a stateless Litwack.

Now what is a Litwack, and how did one become stateless? When I was born shortly before World War I, my parents were in Riga, and my sister and I were therefore Russian citizens. My father then emigrated to Berlin; when the First World War broke out, he was arrested as an enemy and interned for a while by the Germans. Years after the War he became a Latvian citizen, since Riga was then the capital of the recently created Latvian Republic. But they did not give me the Latvian citizenship. The Latvians expected and demanded that I come *home* and go into the Latvian army for two years. I refused because I had no attachment whatsoever to Latvia. So I became stateless in Berlin and remained so ever since.

Now, what about being a Litwack? Jews in Eastern Europe had developed a certain mentality, regionally colored and influenced by the people among whom they lived. There were the Polish Jews who were different in outlook and behavior from the Galizianer or Romanian or Hungarian Jews. A Jew from Odessa (Ukraine) was recognizable in manners and accent (in his Yiddish as well as in his Russian speech) from the Jews of Northern Russia (Riga, Vilna, Kovno). The latter ones were called *Litvacks* because they originated in Latvia or Lithuania. Besides this, though there were famous Jewish Academies (Yeshivoth) all over Russia and Poland, the most famous and most important for Jewish knowledge, thought and Law was the Yeshiva in Vilna, especially during the last few centuries. Since my four grandparents had lived in Vilna (as their parents and grandparents had before them) and then emigrated to Riga, I consider myself basically a Litvack, despite having gone through German Gymnasia and Universities.

But back to Langlade. The tension among us became such that one had to isolate oneself for a while and leave those murky waters of rumors and half cooked reasoning, those ill tempered brush fires of anger and helplessness, for which there is only compassion or pity. Yes, I would have to think of a way to get out of there.

We read between the lines in the newspapers that the British, in doubt about the provisions of the French-German Armistice, had tried to convince the French Admiral of the necessity for the French ships to join the Royal Navy or at least to sail to a port out of reach of the Germans, but they did not succeed. On July 3 the French fleet was attacked at Mers-el-Kebir by the Royal Navy and destroyed. About three hundred French sailors were killed or missing. A hate campaign against Great Britain, the Ally of yesterday, was building up in Wagnerian orchestration and under the slogan: *Never forget Mers-el-Kebir.*

French troops fleeing from the North and the Center were still coming South by the thousands, trying to avoid falling into German hands and being taken prisoners. Marseille—about six hours by train from Langlade—was one of the centers where these military men were still being quickly discharged. Though ours was a military auxiliary group, it was clear by now to everybody that they would never discharge us, but transform us into *concentrationists*.

I had to think of some way out.

Sonia wrote in her last letter that she had met through some friends a lady from Vienna who had asked her to make a dress for her. If it came out alright, there would be more customers. The 300 francs allowance ($20), which she recieved from the military for me, paid for her room. So if she could make a little money with sewing, our meager resources would last longer. To return to German occupied Paris was out of the question for us, though a few had left Langlade clandestinely, somehow crossed the demarcation line at Vierzon and gone home to Paris. By the way, Boris and Paulette, Jeanne and Jacques had not yet left Paris, and lived now under the swastika. What horror.

It was getting increasingly difficult for the French to put something on the table at meal time. For the time being I did not have this worry. Though what they gave us to eat was not enough, we still had a hot soup a day, a piece of bread and a kind of brew in the morning which had only the name *Coffee* left. But with grape harvesting time around the corner, we often went into the fields and ate pounds and pounds of grapes to our heart's delight.

Early in August I heard that discharges from the Army would be issued until August 15. It was clear now that they would not give us a military discharge in Langlade; we would, rather, be allowed to glide graciously from the status of military second class into first class foreign internee. I had ten or twelve days to do some thinking and to come up with something that would facilitate my discharge. Fred Glauberg, a Jew from Frankfort, an engineer and a very ingenious mind, had succeeded in being officially *detached* from Langlade and was sent to some industry in Saint Etienne.

Finally I thought of something a purely legal mind might raise a brow and have a question or two about, but so many of the new laws were built on injustice that we—in our search for survival —tried out some unorthodox ways to get around those inhuman (and German inspired) regulations. The result of my thinking was that I found myself in Nice with my wife, *officially* discharged from the Military Center in Marseille and hoping for the best.

What did Napoleon's mother Laetitia—in her heavy Corsican accent—say about her son's Empire? *Pourvou que ca doure,* meaning: let's hope it will last. Here is what I did.

I had a friend of ours in Nice, a medical man, send me a letter in which he warned about Sonia's nervous state, asking me if I could get a permit to come to Nice for a week or so, so we could discuss the situation. There was still humanity in the office in Langlade. Drucker, the young fellow from Vienna, got me a permission duly signed, and I was off for Nice. When I had to wait two hours in Marseille to get the train, I put my suitcase into a locker, found out where the Military Demobilization Center was and rushed over there. I showed the man my enlistment paper from 1939, my medical examination paper and my presence at the group paper. He had no idea what a prestataire was, and I was in no hurry to explain it to him. I fumbled something about an engineering military labor unit, a recently created outfit. My French—I almost spoke it like a Frenchman—was very helpful. Besides, there were twenty men waiting in line behind me, and he—obviously—was in a hurry and wanted to get rid of me. He gave me the discharge paper, a real military document with stamps and all the rest, and I was off for the Railroad Station. Since Sonia had no telephone, I sent her a telegram, explaining that I had missed my train for a good reason and that I would arrive in Nice around midnight. When I arrived in Nice, there was still a trolleybus that took me up to Avenue Bellanda in Cimiez-Nice.

Sonia was skeptical about my kind of discharge; so was I deep down. There was only one real and legal discharge from Langlade, namely in Langlade itself. But we were living from week to week, from month to month. A month in freedom was a month won.

Though we had been free inside the village of Langlade, though we could even move a few miles to a neighboring village or town, the Camp atmosphere, the environment of strangely uniformed helpless internees, was very depressing and at times unbearable. Here in this big city of Nice not only were the people clothed like civilians, but they tried to move around and to behave as if the War had not been lost, as if the Gestapo was not all over the place, in short: as if nothing had happened. In this make-believe world we tried to integrate knowing that it could not last. But my desire to be out of Langlade was irrepressible.

Nice had always been a city with plenty of retired people who came to live out their last years in the Riviera sunshine. There is little industry, except the perfume and tourist business, both dormant in these days. The foreigners who fled to Nice and who had money were waiting for a visa to the U.S., to Cuba or Santo

Domingo. Those who had no money spent their last few thousand francs before being sent to a Camp, because—as the legal wording goes—they were *unable to prove any means or a livelihood.*

One day we took a long walk from Nice uphill to Cimiez. A beautiful day it was, sunny and pleasant. The streets were almost empty. The sky was a full Mediterranean blue. Suddenly we heard from afar marching songs coming closer, and here they were: about two thousand uniformed militia men, the recently created ultranationalist, pro-German gang of Doriot. You want a good scare? Look at their faces. This is the same breed as the SA (Sturm-Abteilungen) which we had seen on the Kurfurstendamm in Berlin seven years earlier and from which we had fled. They were cruel, brutal, vile, degenerate. What progress did sixty generations of Christians and Jews and all the other decent people fight for, if it came to the reign of the beast in man, of the subhuman that we witnessed in our days?

By the way, speaking about Christians and Jews, the horrible Nuremberg laws based on anti-Semitic persecution had been imposed on Marshal Pétain who did not have the courage or the desire to resist. Is it true that the Revolutionary slogan LIBERTY, EQUALITY, FRATERNITY was but a joke and that we were back to the business of persecuting, tormenting and assassinating innocent people, even in France? It was terrifying to see how a free press could be muzzled and nazified within a few days. The Communist newspaper "L'Humanité" had no effort to make. Since the Molotov-Ribbentrop pact a year ago, the Communists had been consistently against any anti-German War effort and outspokenly pro-Hitler, since Hitler was now a friend of Stalin.

Life, this precious and fragile gift, is always an endangered proposition. For us it had become an extremely perilous path. Every step might bring a catastrophe. There was no response from Langlade as yet. The Nice Police did not arrest me either. Maybe they really would forget me and leave me alone; dreams sometimes come true. We at times have the feeling of not walking on solid ground, but of being suspended by a thread high up in the air. Will I come crushing down? Who knows.

I did come crushing down. I was sent back to Langlade. It was on the 5th of October that a gendarme came to arrest me. The first thing he asked me after my name was to hand over my precious discharge paper. Thank God they did not arrest Sonia, the wife of the criminal who had chosen freedom for a moment. Sonia accompanied us to the Gendarmery Prison in Nice where we were separated. I spent three days in that filthy prison, and on the 8th of October they shipped me back to Langlade. My comrades had a good laugh when they saw me reappear, the sarcastic and spiteful laugh of those who see that the trick of the other fellow did not work. But Sachs, the more intelligent, told them: "What are you laughing about? He had two months vacation at the Riviera, not you".

Things had drastically changed in Langlade. We were not prestataires any more, but *foreign laborers*. The commanding officer, a Captain, and his seargents were gone, replaced by a civilian commander, Theo Bruant, and some civilian assistants, concentration camp types. We still were allowed to live in that old Vieilledent-house, but discipline had become stricter, the soup thinner and the rumors in the air thicker and foreboding.

One persistent rumor had it that we would all soon be sent to the salt mines where we would stand up to the belly in saltwater all day long and shovel salt—which was not a very enticing prospect. There was a way out though, a difficult one. In order to avoid such a transfer and the danger it held for our health, one would have to prove that his presence in Langlade was profitable and useful for the Company. A Czech Jew, a chemist, had opened in Langlade a kind of laboratory with some of his friends. They produced cooking oil out of bones which the Artillery Depot in Nîmes and some big butcheries had so far discarded. Our horse and buggy brought these now precious bones every morning from Nîmes, and our men extracted the oil which the Company sold. Evidently they were spared any transfer to SALT CITY as we called it, but being overstaffed already, they would not take me and my friends in. So I had again to think of something quickly, because the transfer might start in a few days.

Is it not strange. A few weeks ago I was fighting to get out of Langlade because it was about to become a simple concentration camp; now I was fighting to stay in. Torment and worries had been our daily bread for six months now.

Liberty, Equality, Fraternity, the slogan of the French Revolution had been replaced by Petain's WORK, FAMILY, COUNTRY. My thinking started from here. A little water-color, let's say a vineyard—so familiar to our farmers here—or any other pleasant landscape in color, placed into a mat—if it can be cheaply produced, would certainly attract many buyers among those winegrowers. I am an artist, so is Liebknecht the son of Karl Liebknecht (the Communist leader who was assassinated in Germany after World War I); there is the painter Schiff. We could use someone for cutting mats; Schauder with his verbal fluency could go around selling these handmade pictures which would—on the bottom—show the beautiful words WORK, FAMILY, COUNTRY and their author MARSHAL PETAIN. Whatever we would sell, the money we would take in for spreading art and Pétain's slogan among the farmers would go directly to the National Aid Society (Secours National), and—last but not least—we five or six would be saved from the salt mines. The Commandant liked the idea. My good friend in the office, Drucker, spoke out for it. So we were given a chance to show what we could do for the Company, for art, for the Marshal and for the country.

Weingarten cut the water-color paper and the mats; he carried water from the pump. Schauder and Reich were our salesmen, Schauder being a fast talker and Reich a handsome young man. Both were irresistible to men and women. Liebknecht, Schiff and I did the artwork. We sold a picture for frs. 10 and were preparing them by the hundreds.

The first sale day was encouraging. For the time being we did not have to go to the salt mines, but we would have to produce and to sell more to make more money for the Company, i.e. for the National Aid Society. I was desperate not being able to send any money to Sonia, but she wrote that she now had a few customers in Nice for dresses and alterations, so I should not worry. On the contrary, she said, if I did not get enough to eat in Langlade, I should spend a little of our money on myself. I was very moved, but, of course, I did not.

At the end of October they took Weingarten away to the mines. Who will be next? We would have to sell more. So far we sent about frs. 700 to the National Aid Society. We would have to accelerate our production, too, if we wanted to survive in Langlade. It was getting cold and we had no ovens in the rooms, only downstairs in the windowless kitchen where no work was possible. We would have to invent some heating system, but how?

For a few portrait sketches I did of the cook Gelb and his aides I negotiated the purchase of a big oil canister which we brought home. Reich was good with his hands; he produced a little oven from this can. But the problem arose, with what to fire and to heat it. There were no forests in the region. And here Schauder had a splendid idea; it was legally not very adequate, but splendid anyway. (It is good to have a seasoned salesman in the gang.)

At the Langlade Railroad Station there was a dead end rail which had no reasonable function whatsoever. The rail was rusty, but the crossbeams were still good. One such beam would help us over the winter. These beams looked very heavy. We would need four men with solid shoulders to carry them, and no onlookers spreading stupid news in Langlade. Only we three could do it and Sachs would help us.

One night, after 1:00 AM, we unscrewed the farthest beam; it was pointed on one side like a tooth pick. We put our four shoulders, two left and two right, under it, and off we marched. All Langlade is fast asleep at 1:30 AM and we got home with our treasure without any hindrance. Then we began cutting the *toothpick* into small pieces; the saw had seen better days before World War I. What a job, but it warmed us somehow, and we started to burn one piece. What we had not known was that these crossbeams were soaked in petrol; not only did it smell atrociously, but the smoke of it made us cough and could have given us away. Whoever thought of burning a petrol-soaked girder? We would have to solve this problem. At least our fingers were not blue from the cold.

We now had the Germans in France for about five months, and they had left nothing to eat for the population. Even the wine which flowed like water in this part of the country was being rationed. We got used to making our own shapeless cigarettes from brown corn-grass. Rye bread looked and tasted like a muddy mass of potato peels. The white bread had long lost its white color and its crunchy taste. Anyway we would have liked to have more even of this ersatz bread.

The few dozens of our group who were still left in Langlade seemed to settle down and hoped to hibernate in this Godforsaken Languedoc village. We tried to make ourselves useful as *paying guests,* tried not to fall sick—God forbid—and somehow to get through this winter of 1940/41 which began with a terrible coldspell. In the evenings Kczuk sold us a glass of tea for 3 cent. in the large stable, tea for which he made repeated commercial cries

"Tschai—Tschai" (Tschai is the Russian word for tea). We listened to the reports from BBC which Tabatchnik had caught on radio earlier in the day. This was our only contact with the outside world and our source of information about what was going on. Though the Germans jammed the transmissions from London, the four famous notes beginning the Fifth Symphony by Beethoven gave everybody some hope that only a battle was lost, not the war that was now upon us.

5

THINGS WERE GETTING darker and darker. Laval met with Hitler at Montoire on October 22 and agreed wholeheartedly with him that Great Britain had to be defeated. When Pétain met with Hitler two days later, it was not so easy going, because Pétain, at 84, had lost nothing of his cunning, and Hitler seemed to distrust him. Even if Pétain dealt secretly with Great Britain, we would evidently get no word of it on BBC. One thing came through clearly in the London broadcasts: Hitler's bombing of England, so deadly and devastating, did not diminish the British will to fight on. On the contrary, it increased it. The world has a great debt towards England which stood alone in the storm and alone withstood the onslaught. Thank God for a man like Churchill!

Early in November I was called to the Office, this time for some good reason. The Marshal Pétain had written us a letter, thanking us—the group, that is—for the frs. 725,50 which we, the painters, had sent him for the National Aid Society. From the Office and with the letterhead of "Marshal Pétain, Chief of State" we had received a Thank You letter, we the Jews Schiff, Barosin and Liebknecht. I was perplexed. The last one, the son of Karl Liebknecht, was not much of a Jew anymore, and his father, leader of the Communist Party in Germany, shot twenty years ago, would have turned around in his grave had he learned that his son had sent some money to the Nazi-Collaborator Philippe Pétain. There occur ironies in real life that no playwright or novelist could invent. I immediately had two copies of this letter made for me. A letter like this may save a life in danger in these bizarre times.

This letter enhanced and strengthened the position of us poor painters who never had too much prestige in the policies and intrigues of the Office. The Commander was impressed. It seemed that we would stay for the time being in Langlade and might really dig in for the winter. It was now getting bitterly cold. Our big toothpick was very helpful, and we got used to the smell.

Sketching the cook from all sides worked miracles. Once in a while we received a good piece of meat under the table, or a pound of Swiss cheese. Those were our holidays now.

I immediately sent Sonia a copy of Pétain's letter. If her husband is a *friend* of the Marshal, and this Marshal thanks him personally for sending him some money, this fact must impress any civil servant or any employee of the Nice Police. One never knew in those days when it may come in handy. There was only one thing to do: to cling to life, to hang on and not to go under; never mind those innocent detours.

The German military might from Bordeaux to Warsaw was greater than ever in those beginning days of 1941. Some Frenchmen I spoke to shared Laval's view: we have to help the winner win the War. This is the right side to be on. It will only be good for France to jump on the bandwagon right away. But there were many who lowered their heads in shame.

Of course our Commander was on the Laval side; otherwise he would not have gotten the job and all the good food for his wife and six kids. Once we got into a short conversation and I told him frankly that all my life I was inspired by the three splendid concepts of the French Revolution, Liberty, Equality, Fraternity. He had but a sarcastic smile:

"Ah, les trois blagues (still the three jokes). Look where they got you."

"I dont know yet", I answered, "a Jew has a long memory and a lot of patience".

Here our conversation ended abruptly.

The news from those who had been sent to the salt mines was bad. Three already had ended up in the hospital. Which hospital? What was wrong? What kind of care did they receive?

Is there no way to get out of Langlade and to be officially liberated? Some of our boys made it. One was a Rumanian Jew; he was—so to speak— under "the protection" of his government (that had its own anti-Semitic laws). There were at this point only

German and Austrian and a few Czech Jews left. I was the only Russian. They treated us by nationality. Nice was full of Russian Jews, under surveillance, but free. I knew I had to think of some way out, but with this Siberian cold the thinking process began to freeze and to slowly deteriorate.

The simplest physical necessities like a call of nature became a problem in this cold weather. Our Company had built a kind of *toilet*, a five minute walk from our house. Of course it was not a toilet as we knew it in the city. It was a 30 feet long narrow board walk with six holes cut in it and laid over a ditch. Some bushes hid this structure from view. Squatting there, the brown cape around your body protected you poorly against the icy wind. In summer while crouching there you would glimpse a few headlines from your neighbor's newspaper; but now in winter nobody would read his paper there—and there was not much to read in the paper anyway. You would do whatever there had to be done, try not to catch cold and get out as quickly as possible.

The Germans, not keeping their promise, had again annexed Alsace and Lorraine. They had almost emptied the French Treasury and ravaged French industry. They requisitioned most of the food in this agriculturally rich country. As a result we all suffered from undernourishment.

I had a five day permit and spent them with Sonia in Nice. We cried a little bit when we thought about the months and years passing by in misery and mediocrity, not knowing what the future had in store for us. We just lived on, ate, drank, slept and we knew that we should count ourselves lucky if we could go on surviving this horrifying turmoil.

There was a fascinating mixture in Sonia. She was remarkably intelligent, yet still had a childlike quality. She did not make friends easily, because her demands were high and not often met by ordinary standards. She never forgot a hurt. In appearance as well as in shape of mind she was a very noble woman, extremely gifted. Sonia has her place in the innermost recesses of my heart.

Walking through the avenues of beautiful Nice we were even more aware of what privilege it was to spend a few days in civilization, in warmth and affection. How depressing thereafter, when, approaching by train these little hills and naked vineyards near Langlade, I had to get ready, mentally, to return to that Labor Camp.

If the winter went on like this, we would be out of wood pretty soon. I was a little reluctant to go on breaking up the Railroad Station further, even if it was only the dead end of it.

Speaking about a dead end in Langlade, I was given to understand by the people in the Office that a new law may come out soon, a kind of a Christmas gift to foreigners, according to which an internee could be liberated under certain conditions, if the Prefect of a Department (France was divided into eighty departments or provinces) agreed to give him the right to live in one of its cities evidently under surveillance. I did not yet dare to hope that such a law was really in the making, after Vichy just adopted the anti-Semitic Nuremberg laws. The Romans say "Timeo Danaos et dona ferentes". I dread the Danaees, especially when they come up with presents. Something must be brewing behind this generosity, I thought. What did the words *certain conditions* mean, or *surveillance*? Would this be an easier picker-upper, in case they needed Jews for some nefarious purpose, and at the same time saving the money for their upkeep in Camps? We would soon see.

I was glad to hear that Sonia had an interzonal postcard from Paris in which Jeanne wrote that she had gone into our apartment, seals or no seals, and got the violin which she now had in her possession. Good old Jeanne. Sonia was so happy that her violin was saved, for the time being. Was it another good omen? We did not know what would happen to the apartment and the furniture, but didn't care now about those things when our health, our very lives carried such a big question mark.

In a mere six months, civilized France had turned into an occupied satellite of Nazi-Germany. What a nightmare.

Fred Glauberg who had shared our protracted existence in Langlade for a short while and who had befriended me at that time, had been detached and had moved to St. Etienne where his chemical knowledge and his vast imagination seemed to be greatly appreciated. I received a card from him, asking how long I *intended* to stay in Langlade. With the wine harvest over, Langlade in his opinion must not have much attraction any more. How right he was. He asked me to say hello to Mr. Charles Couton in Clarensac, mayor of that village, about two miles away. What he meant was: go over to see Mr. Couton in Clarensac; maybe he can do something to get you out of Langlade.

So I went. I put on my dark gray suit, the only good one left, a clean blue shirt and a tie, and a pair of civilian shoes. The mayor's villa was one of the first houses of Clarensac. I opened the wooden gate, walked up the five or six steps and found myself in a little frontyard in which a beautiful house stood. A big barking Labrador was held at its collar by a tall, gray haired man, about sixty years of age. He stood at the entrance door, waved to me with a smile and asked me to come in. I was led into a large room, a *salon* (living room) with beautiful antique furniture and rugs and a fire in a huge open fire place. These things apparently still did exist. I introduced myself, mentioning that in a letter my friend Glauberg had asked me to bring his kind regards to which I might be allowed to add my best Christmas wishes.

"Ah, that's very kind of you. Why don't you sit down, Mr."

"Barosin."

"Oh, yes, Mr. Barosin. Hmm. Can I offer you a drink?"

"Thank you, Mr. Mayor," I said rather formally. "I am not in the habit of drinking so early in the day. I came, sir, to make your acquaintance. Glauberg told me so much about you and Mrs. Couton."

"He is quite a fellow. He is in St. Etienne, I believe". He turned to asking about me. "What is your profession, Mr. Barosin, are you a chemist too?"

"No, I am an art historian and a painter. Unfortunately I have not done anything in either field for quite a while."

"Art historian?" He seemed genuinely interested. "That should interest my daughter who visits all the old churches around here. Not me, you can believe that." Mayor Couton called out: "Yvonne, Yvonne . . ."

Here came Yvonne. She was well built, with a happy smile and the black eyes of Southern France, intelligent looking. A pretty woman.

The mayor made the introduction, telling his daughter: "You know, Mr. Barosin, who stays in Langlade, is an art historian and a painter."

"Oh," she said, "then you are in the right place in this region to study Romanesque and Gothic country architecture." What a friendly voice she had.

"I know," I replied. "Though except for Calvisson, Arles, St. Gilles and, of course, Avignon, I have not seen much. I'm not at freedom to do a lot of traveling, you know. Naturally, I have been in Nîmes a few times and have seen the Pont du Gard. But those are Roman monuments, gigantic, fantastic, and I am not an archaeologist."

"Is not the Palace of the Popes in Avignon a grandiose structure?" Yvonne asked enthusiastically.*

"It's almost overwhelming," I agreed. "I once had a few hours to visit it and to look at the murals. You have certainly seen the Simone Martini paintings."

"Oh, yes."

"I mention them because I have especially worked on Siennese Art of which Simone Martini is one of the greatest. Then, later, I did research on the 16th century in Siena, with emphasis on the Mannerist School centering around Domenico Beccafume."

She did not know that name, but she was polite. "How interesting. Where did you study, Mr. Barosin?"

"In Berlin. I graduated from Freiburg University, just in time before Hitler came to power. Being a Jew, I would not have been allowed to finish my studies after 1933, especially since I am not a German, but an ex-Russian citizen."

"Yes," Mayor Couton cut in, perhaps a bit bored by the conversation. "We Frenchmen follow with the greatest shame the events that afflicted our country and we look at the near future with anxiety."

Yvonne took the hint from her father. "I am sorry." she smiled, "but I have some urgent work in the house. It has been a great pleasure meeting you, Mr. Barosin, and we hope to see more of you . . . and of your sketches."

"How kind of you, Mrs. Roche-Couton," I said. I really thank you very much."

She left.

"Where were you born, Mr. Barosin"? the mayor asked.

"I am an ex-Russian citizen."

"Then this is not a place for you; there are mostly Germans and Austrians in Langlade, as far as I know."

"Exactly," I said seriously. "And that's what I keep telling the commanding officer and the office people, but to no avail."

*During a schism in the Roman Catholic Church there were two papacies, one of which was seated in Avignon.

"How long have you been here now?"

"All the six months since June, with a short interruption which I spent in Nice with my wife."

"Listen well, Mr. Barosin," the mayor said firmly. "The Prefect in Nîmes is a friend of mine. I heard him talk the other day about a possible liquidation of your group. An indiscreet question now: Do you have some means, so you would not have to live at the expense of the Authorities?"

"Yes, for about a year and a half or two," I improvised. It was an exaggeration.

"That's just fine," he said. "Let me talk to Louis. But first bring me copies of your identity papers, all of them. I will give you a letter of recommendation to the Prefect, and maybe you could settle in Nîmes. You understand that I cannot promise anything, but I will do my best to get such a nice fellow off the hook."

He stood up. So did I. I was flushed in the face and my hand was trembling when I grasped his and shook it firmly. In the Russian manner I would have embraced him, but I resisted that impulse. On the steps that led to the street I turned around.

"Bring me your papers, Barosin," he said again.

"I certainly will, Mr. Mayor."

I did not know how I got home to Langlade. Probably I flew; there was no ground under my feet. I told nobody about the subject of our conversation because I did not want to hear any discouragement or envy or irony. I just told them that I visited a Frenchman in Clarensac, to whom I was recommended by Glauberg.

"Aha, General Glauberg," Schauder laughed and went on with his solitaire.

What a beautiful living room some people live in, I thought, and for the first time in a long time I noticed the stench coming from our so-called fire place. At 3 PM I had a nice talk with Drucker in the office who promised to make copies of my identity papers for me and to have them ready two days from now. Then I wrote a letter to Sonia. I toned my excitement down, as not to get her expectations too high, but I gave her a detailed report of my conversation with my new elderly friend.

6

THEN CAME CHRISTMAS 1940. There was little joy in so many homes, since France had been defeated, and more than a million Frenchmen were still prisoners in Germany.

Shortly thereafter I went to see Mr. Couton in Clarensac to bring him the copies of my identity papers. He was very kind, introduced me to his wife, a distinguished, very well dressed lady, and we three had a nice conversation. I had to tell them about my background, my family, and everything seemed to interest them. They accepted my small present, a bottle of Muscat wine which I had unearthed somewhere in Langlade.

"You understand, my friend," the mayor laid his hand upon my shoulder, "that during the Christmas week nothing much can be done; but during the first week in January I promise you to get busy and to see what the result will be."

I thanked him and his wife for their great kindness, and left about twenty minutes after I had shown up.

On the winding road back to Langlade I tried to get a clearer picture of this Southerner. Would he be able to keep his word, or did his imagination run away with him quicker than his real possibilities justified? Maybe I should not exaggerate his opportunities or his influence, though his good will was beyond doubt. In my situation I was prone, naturally, to grasp at any hopeful sign or promise.

There was something else. Since he had asked during my first visit whether I had any means, I had better ask Sonia to get some kind of letter or certificate from our friends indicating that they held in trust something like frs. 20.000 for us; this sum would appear to be sufficient to live very modestly for about a year.

The days passed, and the weeks ... The only thing that filled our days were the "Work, Family, Country" pictures that kept us busy for a few hours—and, of course, our endless worries. Or a walk to a neighboring village, whenever the cold let up a bit. At the end of January 1941 I had a short letter from Mr. Couton indicating that he was working on my case, that those things moved slowly, but that I should not lose courage if red tape took a little more time than we all wished. He did prefer not to put his name and address on the envelope. Of course not. A French Mayor corresponding with a foreign internee! That's almost treason.

In Langlade we were getting on each other's nerves. I tried to keep my cool as much as I could. Some, with their bad or tempestuous character, just could not take this insecurity and this misery any longer. There were arguments all the time, even fights. We were all undernourished, had been away from our families for long months worrying about them. Any small reason was good enough for an explosion. A Math Professor from the Vienna University got into a bloody fight over a bread end which he considered his due. And we others watched the fight. There was so little entertainment in Langlade.

Mrs. Sachs became pregnant. What courage! They had an 8-year-old girl, a charming child. Now Mrs. Sachs expected her second child early in summer. There was no doctor in Langlade, no French licensed one anyway. For medical care she had to go to Nîmes. Is it courage or irresponsibility?

Pétain had fired Laval last December at the risk of displeasing the Germans. He did it because Laval wanted war against England and a transfer of the French Colonies in Africa to Hitler. The Germans, therefore, broke off all negotiations about the release of French prisoners in Germany. Flandin, who replaced Laval, had a hard time with the occupying power. Radio London told us that he was being completely ignored by the Germans. The Demarcation Line that separated the two parts of France was tightened and it became increasingly difficult to get a safe-conduct pass from the Germans to cross it.

Spring was now not far away. Time—dangerous and threatening —was dragging on. During all these weeks I had heard nothing from Mr. Couton. I was getting impatient. So I decided to take the bull by the horns and I went there early in March. Nothing. Zero. He was very friendly, as usual, so was his wife—who came out for a moment—but a bit embarrassed. He gave me good advice, though, which turned out to be decisive. He suggested that I write to three or four Prefects in the South, e.g., the Prefects of the Departments of Herault, Lozere, etc., and whoever responded favorably, into his Department I should move. After all, the main thing for me was to get out of that straight-jacket of Langlade. According to him, nothing was final yet in the Prefecture of the Gard (in Nîmes), but he handed me my identity papers—which told me enough. Of course, I thanked him for all he had done or had tried to do for me, and I told him that if and whenever I would be successful in regaining my freedom, he would be the first one to know.

I rushed home to begin my letter writing. Drucker in the office agreed to give me two more sets of my identity papers. Despair should not gain the upper hand: I remembered a teacher in school who had hammered into our heads the motto: Never, ever give up!

Schauder disclosed his secret to me: namely, he had asked for a residence permit in Nîmes. No answer either. He showed me his new visiting card: "R. Schauder, Industrialist". This together with a padded curriculum vitae may impress any Prefect. I think Schauder had a little lumber shop back home. But Schauder is a very good salesman and has a lot of imagination to communicate.

It was time to go to Nice. My nerves were at a low. I sent out my letters to the Prefects; answers may come in a fortnight. I had to get away from it all.

Sonia looked better this time. She had a few good friends in Nice: Mrs. Hirsch from Vienna, an elderly couple from Germany, Misha and Liza who had not yet left for the U.S.A. All those refugees in Nice lived like in a fairy tale, in a make believe world (with afternoon coffee and croissants in a coffee house), where a very important dimension, namely reality, had been skipped, because it wasn't pleasant enough.

As I left for Nice our good cook Gelb gave me a huge piece of cheese, at least a pound and a half, and a steak big enough for three meals for us. Sonia had not seen such treasures for a long time. She had the feeling, she said, that something good would come out of my Prefecture applications for residency, and that we would be together again soon. Her premonitions were often right, so I tried desperately to hold on to them, and did not show her how low my morale was.

By the way, it was this elderly couple from Berlin (the husband had been a big shot at the UFA, the great movie concern) who had given Sonia the frs. 25.000 letter. What a magnificent invention, my new fortune, and I could not thank him enough.

Besides rumors that the Italians, profiting from the downfall of France, would recover Nice (which had once been theirs), everything was quiet and everybody was hungry in Nice.

One beautiful day in April 1941 I was called to the Office. Hurrah. There was a favorable decision from the Prefect of Herault (Capital Montpellier) saying that under certain conditions I could take residence in his Department, the city to be determined later. The conditions were:

1) I had not been punished for a misdemeanor or theft etc. during my stay in Langlade.

2) Proof of possessing the means to live independently and seeking no job, except in Agriculture.

3) A legalized discharge from the Group of Foreign Workers in Langlade.

Hurrah again. I had become practically a free man over night. All these conditions were easy to fulfill. But I was not out yet. Things might still go wrong at the last minute; here I needed the good will of the Commandant and the people in the Office.

Schauder had been freed and had already moved to Nîmes; I was so glad for him. With Weingarten and Schauder gone (Reich had returned to Paris) I lived alone in that old house, with nothing to do and almost nobody to talk to. The nights had become real nightmares again with all those bedbugs that had multiplied by the hundreds. What will become of me? Why were they dragging their feet now in the Office? They had promised to send out the necessary papers for me; had they really done it?

I rushed over to my new friends, the Couton's in Clarensac. They were both overjoyed and they showed it; they both embraced me. We had a little drink with Mrs. Couton's excellent cookies, and I promised them that I would let them know as soon as I knew where I would live. Would my wife come from Nice to stay with me? Of course, this brought a standing invitation to Clarensac.

A letter came from Sonia overflowing with joy. She almost could not believe that this painful nightmare was coming to an end.

Neither could I myself. Since good things come in pairs my letter with the good news had come to her on the same day that Jacques — her cousin — had sent her frs. 4.000 from Paris. She had thanked Jacques and Jeanne immediately. I sent a card of thanks myself through the interzonal post. Here my War debts began and they continued to increase during the following years.

I did not yet know how we would manage to live wherever that good Prefect of Herault would send us, but those are things we worried about later. For the time being: Finished Langlade, finished Langlade. It was difficult to grasp. But for some reason my liberation was delayed. Every day I went to the office; no answer from the Herault Prefect. Drucker assured me that my papers had gone out six days ago. There were new rumors: Those who could should get out of Langlade quickly. The Company would be dissolved in the very near future.

Finally, on May 15th, I was a free man. It would be difficult to find words for my excitement and joy.

The Prefect of Herault gave me the right to live in Lunel. Lunel, with ten thousand inhabitants, is located exactly in the middle between Nimes and Montpellier, 23 km. from each of these big cities. I had the permit papers with all those administrative stamps and signatures in my possession. This piece of paper meant Freedom for me.

I asked the Commandant for a permit to Nice. Sonia invited some of the ladies, and we had a little freedom celebration in Nice, exactly one year after our arrest in Paris. What a disastrous year it had been. France was defeated; Hitler victorious. All of Europe, Central Europe that is, with France, Poland and Italy were German by now. Spain, Switzerland and Sweden remained — so to speak — neutral and unoccupied. Russia was the great question mark. Radio London told of German troop concentrations and a military buildup in Poland, near the Russian border, but there was nothing in the French papers.

I was so happy to be with my wife that I overstayed my furlough in Nice by one day. But I left for Lunel the next day. I had to find a room there and to see how things would work out. I was not allowed to stay any longer in Nice, though I would have preferred it. I had no residence right there and they could have arrested me as they had tried to do with Sonia in Langlade. I did not want to overplay my card in Nice; in Lunel I could legally stay for the time being, with this glorious Prefecture paper in hand.

I left Nice on May 21. Sonia soon wrote that three days later a gendarme had shown up at her place to arrest me. Nice had been advised by my Commander that I had a permit only until the 20th and could be picked up any time thereafter. The policeman was a decent fellow and said that he was glad that I had left and that he did not have to arrest me. I would have been sent to a real Concentration Camp.

With a change of trains it took about an hour from Langlade; by car it would be twenty minutes to Lunel. A new chapter began. I left my suitcase at the Station and walked through the streets of this ancient town. In the center the streets became narrower and crooked; some had low arcades. Here was an old shapeless square, surrounded by houses and facades that were built centuries and centuries before our time. This was France of the early Middle Ages, a whole city like a museum piece, whose strange and remarkable history I did not yet know at this point.

7

THE SUN WAS out, it was 5 or 5:30 PM and I walked through the streets to find a *Room for rent* sign. There was none. So I asked people if they knew of somebody in the neighborhood who would like to take in a roomer. The first two I asked did not know of any. But the third, a nice young woman with a broom in her hand told me that Augustine, around the corner, had said not long ago that she would take in a decent roomer if she could find one. I rushed over to 23, Rue Sadi Carnot. Augustine was not in, but her husband Eugene was. He was a young fellow, about my age, with an easy smile. He asked me to sit down in that large kitchen and had a few questions about me. Was I married? What was I doing in Lunel? If *Nothing much yet* (according to my answer), why in Lunel? So I had to unwrap the whole story. Ten minutes later Augustine arrived with her two little boys André and Roger. She was in her thirties. Hard work was showing on her hands and face.

"Andre, Roger, shake hands with Monsieur." They did, a bit embarrassed.

"Well, it isn't much of a room" Augustine started out, "but the bed is good, there is a large chest, and I will see to it that the water is brought into the room every morning. The outhouse is just behind the house in the yard, and the price is frs. 150 a month ($10)."

"Could I see the room?" It must be better than Langlade, I thought.

"Of course. It's on the second floor."

"We all walked up the stairs. I followed Augustine, Eugene followed me and the two little boys, as an indispensable rear, followed their father. The room was all I needed, about twelve by fifteen feet, with a large window to the street. It had a small night table and a lamp, so I could read in the evening. Perfect. I gave her the frs. 150, and I had the clear impression that all five of us were very pleased with the deal, including Andre and Roger, who were 7 and 5. Eugene asked me for my suitcase receipt; he would pick it up with his tricycle and bring it home.

Their name was Salles. He had started out as a butcher, but could not find any work right now because there was nothing to butcher. So he tried his hand at all kind of jobs and was making a great effort to feed his little family in these hard times.

I had a new home. For a full year I had been interned. It seemed strange, at first, recovering your freedom, being on your own and deciding for yourself where to go and what to do. One thing I knew I had to do: find some work, any work. It would not take long until my money would run out. Lunel was a small, sleepy city without any industry to speak of. But I was not allowed to take a job; even the paintings which I would do could not be sold. It would be looked upon by the Authorities as a business, a commerce. And then, frankly, there were no customers in Lunel. There was only one kind of work to which the French admitted foreigners at that time: agricultural work, farm-hand jobs. I had never done it before, but I would, if I could find an employer. Only, watch out: You got your liberation with that frs. 25,000 letter, proving that you are a capitalist. How would that fit in with a farmhand job?

I had a long talk with my new friend Eugene. He himself was looking for something like that in and around Lunel. I asked him not to tell anybody that I was looking for work because of my non-existing frs. 25,000 which the Authorities now expected me to spend (before they would put me into another camp). My God, it was certainly not easy to be a Jew, especially not a foreign or a stateless one—and pennyless at that—during these desperate times in France.

The baker, a few blocks from our house, told me that a friend of his in St. Just (a village about five km. from Lunel) was looking for a farmhand for a part time job. That would be just for me. I asked Eugene if he wanted it, but it did not pay enough for him.

Hitler attacked the Soviet Union on June 22, 1941. The fate of Napoleon in Russia did not deter him. This was Hitler's fatal mistake; we sensed it right away. Much later we learned that

Churchill went down on his knees when he heard of Hitler's attack against the Russians, knowing that Hitler would lose the War, and that Great Britain would be saved.

The German offensive broke all records for speed and breadth. The Russians had given Napoleon's Army a little heat by burning Moscow to the ground, but the Germans would not be treated to that. I am going too fast; we are now in July 1941. The Germans were already overstretching their supply lines.

A propos supply lines: for two weeks I had been working, half a day, at the Dussel farm in St. Just. It took me an hour to walk there and an hour to come back. There was no other way to get there, no bus, no bicycle. I worked in their vegetable garden—which was not so difficult—fed the chickens for an extra bonus of an egg once in a while, and helped Roger Dussel in all kinds of rural jobs. Roger was not a peasant. He was a painter like me who had gone through the School of Fine Arts in Paris, a friendly young man—a bit older than I—and I felt completely at home with him, knowing that he would not betray me for working without official papers. He paid me with a bagful of vegetables, a good piece of bread and frs. 15 for half a day ($1), and, once a week, fruit and an egg or two. I could live on that and have my afternoons for the Library. The Library of the City of Lunel in the City Hall was a delight.

When we think of World War II, we think of the Holocaust, of mass murder and crime, and this is what it was, beginning in 1942. In January 1942, the German government decided during the infamous Wannsee Conference (near Berlin) on the *Final Solution* of the Jewish question, which meant the assassination of every Jewish man, woman and child. They succeeded in annihilating six million out of a nation of eighteen million; six million who lived in the Americas were unreachable to them. However in 1941 and especially in civilized nations like France, Holland, Denmark and Italy where we later received help and shelter from the population, these gruesome developments were still in the future.

That is why life in Lunel in 1941 may seem bucolic and peaceful to the reader. For instance, my greatest worry that summer was the problem how to bring my wife to Lunel and how to support her under all those restrictive conditions. With my sort of income there was no question of having Sonia come to Lunel soon. In Nice she had a few customers for sewing dresses and making alterations; she could make ends meet in a big city like Nice. In Lunel she could not have found a sufficient number of customers, and the secret that she was working would not have been kept for long. There was a complete difference of opinion and intention between the Prefect and us. He wanted us to spend frs. 25.000 in his department, and we not only did not have these frs. 25.000, but we wanted to make a living. I did not know how to bridge this difference and how to solve my problem, but I would have to think of and come up with something, so we could finally live together in the same city.

There was hunger now in Fance due to the constantly increasing demands of the voracious Germans; hunger in a country which had been one of the most blessed and richest agricultural producers in Europe. A black market and cheating were direct consequences of the German occupation. Among other things I helped my friend in St. Just to put three bags of grain away into a secret, undisclosed storage compartment and to hide them there. We were all together in this fight against a pitiless and criminal enemy.

At the end of August began the grape harvest, the "vendanges", and I was a porter in Dussel's vast vineyards. The grapes in the South of France—for hundreds of miles—grow on short trees, three feet high, which spread in all directions and look like bushes. These tree-bushes are planted at a certain distance from each other and follow the most delightful lines and patterns. Each of the ten harvesters, mostly women, had a cylindric pail, about twenty inches in diameter, to put the grapes in. Then we, the three men, placed the thirty or forty pounds on our shoulder or lower neck to carry these pails to the nearby wagon and empty them in it. One of the men carried the pails on his head, as I later saw Arab and African women do. I could not, my head was not solid enough for this kind of work. The advantage of the harvest was that you could eat as many grapes as you wanted.

There was another aspect to harvest time, a romantic one, the Breughel-like happiness of this countryfolk. The women did not mind a hearty slap on their stuck out buttocks and acknowledged this clearly manifested male interest with a reproachful gesture, but with a large smile. Some even, after work in the fields, coupled up for a nice walk, got out of sight and waited for the dark to get home, I was told. It was good in those times of predicaments and dangers to forget for a while the ditch we were all in, to laugh and to tell a joke and to eat grapes to your heart's delight. With all this the weather was glorious. The sun was compassionate and did not mind warming even this undeserving turbulent little globe.

One day in August, before the harvest, Dussel took me in his car to Nîmes, to help him load some heavy material, and I found in an Art shop—from under the table—some tubes of oil paint and a few brushes. It is amazing how conscientious and total German thievery had been in this country. From Rockefort cheese down to painter's canvas and brushes everything had disappeared. Roger Dussel told me that he would show me how to prepare a sheet of plywood for oil painting, and he did. His own paintings showed skill and talent, but they were still swimming in the impressionistic ocean of vagueness and uncontrolled let-go. I began a landscape, a pond with trees in the outskirts of Lunel, on a small panel. Plenty of gypsies lived around Lunel; their children were lovely—I sketched a lot of them.

In the late afternoons I did some reading in the Library at City Hall and, among others, I found there a most interesting book on the *History of the City of Lunel* by Th. Millerot. According to him and to Joury, Lunel was founded around 68 A.D. by Jews who escaped from Judea and from Roman occupation. The Jewish War against the Power of Rome, watched by all the subdued nations, lasted almost four years and ended with the destruction of Jerusalem and the Jewish State by Titus in 70 A.D. Jesus had died about forty years before. Those Jews, about 1900 years ago, came from Jericho: *Jericho* meaning month or moon in Aramaic, they called their new town in Southern France LUNA, Latin for moon. The Romans had conquered Gaul (Caesar) 120 years earlier. During the Middle Ages, when all this region was utterly barbaric, famous Jewish Academies flourished in Lunel, and great Rabbis of that city were in contact with the Academies in Montpellier, Troyes, Reims and with those in the Rhineland. The famous Maimonides mentions Rabbi Jonathan of Lunel in his extraordinary *Guide to the Perplexed,* in the 12th century. All this made Lunel even more attractive to me, it meant a kind of symbolic homecoming.

There was a danger in this bucolic life, and though I enjoyed it for the time being, especially after the dangers and tensions of Langlade, I knew that I should not be lulled into this pseudo-existence, and that this routine was not good enough for me.

We learned that some Frenchmen fought now with the Germans against the Russians. Pétain could not avoid having thousands of his young countrymen sent to work in German factories as *volunteers* in order to help German War production. Pretty soon Frenchmen would go into hiding in their own country to escape the draft into *volunteer-ship*.

Furthermore we heard on Radio London that Admiral Darlan had agreed last spring to let the Germans pass through Syria—a French colony—so they could get to Iraq and take it from the British. Vichy-France supplied arms and instructors to the pro-Nazi Iraqi underground. Fine bedfellows. As an extra bonus the anti-Jewish Mufti of Jerusalem who had visited Hitler in Berlin kept openly haranguing his pious crowd to come over to the Nazis. Darlan, I heard, opened Tunisia to the Germans on their way to Egypt. Would Palestine be occupied by the Germans? Impossible.

Nothing much happened in Lunel. Week after week passed, and I was still alone. I knew that I should be happy to be out of Langlade, but what kind of life is this. Winter had come. Augustine always put a hot brick wrapped in an old towel into my bed which helped, since there was no heat in the room. They were really good people, these Salles. How often did they share their meals with me which made me a member of the family; and I gave them the little money I had. At times I took Andre and Roger for a walk or played with them, and they loved it. Eugene had a hard time finding work; there was no construction, there was no industry in Lunel. Next spring, on his little piece of land outside the city, we would grow vegetables together, and we would have all the vegetables we want during the summer. But how to get over the winter? My job with Dussel came to an end early in winter.

The United States entered the War after Pearl Harbor. We heard the news from London. It was not long before the Germans would have a war on two fronts. However, the Americans came into a World War when they were industrially and organizationally ready. During 1914-18 they came in three years later, in 1917. If they declared war on Japan in now 1941, and Germany declared war on the U.S.A. and their Allies, the US would not come into action before 1944, not in France that is. Would we still be around, I thought, to rejoice in the victory? Only God knows.

8

THE POLICE OFFICER in Lunel in charge of safe conducts for foreigners looked like a decent fellow. He gave me a safe-conduct to go to Nice for six days, so I could spend five days with Sonia, and what a joy it was to interrupt my gray life of forced residence in Lunel. We turned our problems over from A to Z and from Z to A, and we decided that we would have to go through the winter where we were: she in Nice and I in Lunel. She could make a living with her alterations and even put a tiny bit of money aside. If everything went well and I could start my farmhand job with Dussel, working in the afternoon with Eugene in our vegetable garden, Sonia could come to Lunel around Easter 1942 and stay with me there. We would become vegetarians, it is true, but there was nothing wrong with that. I would have to find another room because the small room in the Salles' apartment (without a water pump and without toilet) would not do for the two of us. There were fewer and fewer foreigners left in Nice; most had departed for the United States or Cuba. Those who were still there tried to get transportation on a boat, almost any boat.

The food situation in Nice was deplorable. I went with Sonia to her grocery store in Cimiez; all they had were turnips, and they sold us only two of this delicacy. Sonia cooked them; I have eaten better meals in my life. I was sure I could feed her better in Lunel.

As I said before: to be stateless, protectionless and moneyless —a kind of outlaw—under the Vichy government put us into a very precarious situation, and it would take all our courage, our strength and know-how plus a lot of luck to survive the dangers that hung constantly over our heads. From September 1939 when the War had broken out thirty months had passed. The luxury of earnest intellectual and artistic work was a memory far removed. We were down to the basics of filling our stomachs, not catching cold, and in general, keeping our body warm and healthy.

The winter of 1941/42 was slow and lazy. There were some events to strengthen our hopes: The Germans had their first taste of the Russian winter, and they did not like it. Their offensive was being slowed down and later came to a catastrophic halt for them in Stalingrad. Rommel's retreat in North Africa could not be embellished by excuses and semantics. The U.S. with her unimaginable potential had entered the War a few months ago. Darlan had replaced Laval in Vichy, and even he had now second thoughts about Hitler's victory. So he tried to resist German demands, except in areas unimportant to him like the question of foreign Jews. But at least Vichy refused to send 150,000 French workers into German factories.

Eugene was often nervous those days; and when he was in a bad mood, he screamed at Augustine, and the two little ones kept prudently out of his way. He had a promise from somebody for a three week job, and now he was told that there was no job. His bicycle tires were flat and could not be repaired any more because the patches had holes now. Forget about new ones, there was not such a thing. How would he go out to look for a job? I offered him a little money in case he found some still usable, second hand tires. Oh, misère de misère.

To read the newspaper was a deplorable sport. It was as if we read a Goebbels newspaper in the French language. Everything was under censorship: press, mail, telephone. It was painful to see what could become of a country where freedom once reigned, when the heavy boot of a cruel dictatorship smashed it. How fragile and rare is freedom on this Earth.

This coming summer things should be easier when we would get vegetables from our garden. Our dreams now concentrated on peas, green beans, potatoes, eggplants, some corn and berries. The old Jewish joke came to my mind of two eternally hungry men who met one day. One tells the other that last week he had been invited by rich people for dinner.

"Guess what they served. First there was a marvelous chicken soup. I could have two helpings. Then we had gefillte fish (stuffed fish), rice, potatoes. You bet, I did help myself. After that came chicken, but what a chicken, with peas and salad."

The friend looks on wide-eyed, not to miss one of the dishes.

"And before fruit salad we had stuffed derma (gefillte kishkes)."
Here the listener interrupts him . . .

"Say it once more—Gefillte kishkes." He could not resist the
pleasure of at least hearing the magic words once more. The same
way we were talking about and making plans for those precious
vegetables which you could not get anywhere anymore, neither in
the open market nor a grocery store.

I told the Salles that after Easter I would not be able to stay with
them anymore. They asked among their friends and neighbors, if
anybody knew about a room, if possible with a W.C. And they
came up with a Madame Germain, the widow of a Lunel policeman
who owned a small house on Avenue de Mauguio (for the old
Roman city of Melgorium) in Lunel. Mrs. Germain lived there with
her teenage daughter Jeanne, and she would be willing to take in a
quiet couple. She would even agree to let us use her kitchen at
certain hours.

If everything went according to plan, Sonia would be in Lunel at
the end of March. I had rented the room in Mrs. Germain's house.
She was a nice and friendly woman; her daughter was a little short
for her seventeen years, but she was a bright girl. It was a clean,
large room with two windows to the street, well furnished—com-
paratively, that is—and with the W.C. just across the corridor that
divides the house into two equal parts. The price was frs. 200 a
month. I did not even bargain as is often my oriental habit. I gave
her frs. 100 and told her that we would move in, my wife and I,
about the 1st of April and that she would have no worry with our
paying the rent accurately before the first of each month.

The Salles were a little sad about my leaving; I had become a
member of the family; but friends we will always be. I like simple
folks when they are honest, have a fair portion of horse sense and a
good heart. Sophistication, in my dictionary, is not far from Stupidity and is always coupled with arrogance.

I had a few good days painting gypsy children. Two or three
water colors looked good to me. Sometimes when the weather
allowed it, I was "landscaping" around Lunel.

Sonia arrived in Lunel the 3rd of April. We met her at the
station, i.e. Augustine and the inseparable two little boys with their
bouquet of flowers. Sonia looked fine, a little pale, well dressed as
always—maybe a little to well for Lunel; we left the two suitcases at the station. Eugene had promised to bring them over to

our new place a little later. We walked through Railroad Avenue and got to Mrs. Germain's house just when the sun was setting. The meeting with Mrs. Germain and her daughter went very well. Sonia liked the room too.

Everything seemed so exciting, though the town with its 10.000 people, the crooked streets and the miniature stores was a far cry from Nice, which she had gotten used to after almost two years.

For the evening meal we went to Eugene and Augustine who had prepared a *lapin au vin*, rabbit with wine sauce, a thing that Sonia had never eaten. She tried to make the Salles comfortable with her, though at the beginning the social distance seemed unbridgeable. But goodness of heart appealed directly to her intelligence, and the ice was broken, especially after the meal when she could play with the children.

The morning after her arrival I got up very early because I had to walk to my place of work in St. Just. The chickens, probably knowing that the Germans are voracious egg eaters, but that the people of France have to eat, too, increased their production to a point where even Mrs. Dussel, a dark-eyed little Basque woman, whose lack of generosity was not her least fault, handed me two eggs that day, a kind of welcome present for my wife, and a jar of last year's tomatoes. Needless to say that I worked like a beaver to show my appreciation.

Eugene and I started in April to dig up the soil in *our* future vegetable garden which is a rather big piece of land for four hands. I would say a hundred by hundred fifty feet. We first prepared the soil for the seeds. Fortunately there was a pump, but we had to carry the two pails from pretty far, and after a while it tired you out. The peas and the beans were soon in and the sticks for the plants to climb on, too. It did not take long and tiny tomatoes were showing. And then the day came when it was green all over. Eugene who knew every tree in the region showed me an apple tree that belonged to no one. So I helped myself and brought home at least ten pounds of yellow apples. For Sonia all this abundance was new.

From Boris came a card from Paris, in the cryptic style of persecuted people, saying that Sonia's cousins (that is he and his brother Jacques) would have to give their full names soon (meaning: will have to register as Jews), but that they were too busy to do so. What he wanted to say was, "don't register when they ask you to."

What did the Germans have in mind, asking the Jews to register? What for? From London we got no information on that subject. Did I do the right thing to bring Sonia to this small city of Lunel, where there is no hiding place in case of need? Nice is a big city, and one can always find an attic or a cellar in the house of friends. Boris's card was like an ominous dark cloud that said: Watch out.

Sonia woke up the other morning with hundreds of tiny spots on her face, like needle points. We rushed to the doctor. He said it came from undernourishment, she needed more fat. The dots would disappear in time, he promised. Where could I find some butter for her?

Radio London informed us that 15,000 Jews had been arrested in Paris in July and sent to a concentration camp in Drancy, a suburb of Paris. From there they were transported to an unknown place in an Eastern direction, possibly Germany or maybe even further, men, women and children of all ages. This could not be for work in armament factories to relieve Germans whom they needed for the front in Russia, for the simple reason that they took children and very old people, too. The Germans called it *resettlement.*

Our government in Vichy—under German pressure—had been forced to fire Darlan and to call back Laval who was worse. He believed in a German victory and would do everything they asked him to do. He would certainly not resist, when they asked him to deliver the Jews in France; he would be glad to oblige his masters if he could get some temporary relief for France; and very few would protest.

Rommel was being beaten back in North Africa. The British air attacks were becoming devastating for German industrial centers and cities. The German advance was slowed down by the Soviets, their assault lines being overextended. We heard from London that the U.S. was building up a tremendous War machine, unimaginable for Europeans, part of which would soon come to assist the British. When would they come to liberate suffocating Europe? I hope it won't be too late for us. The wildest rumors were circulating.

The end of August and September was harvest time. We worked at Dussel's farm. He even gave us a room in his house where the two of us stayed for over three weeks. They were really kind and warm people. I had talked to him about a hiding place in his house, in case of deportation of Jews from the so-called Free Zone. He said he would talk to his wife after the harvest.

Sonia's face was clean again, the spots had totally disappeared. Augustine's sister who worked in a grocery store was our doctor this time . . . with some butter under the table, and better results.

In order to change the atmosphere and to forget for a few hours our fears, we went to Nîmes—which is less than a half hour train ride East of Lunel. Nîmes is a large city compared to Lunel with 100,000 inhabitants and its famous Roman Square House (La Maison Carrée) which is one of the rare intact ancient temples, beautifully proportioned, a treasure of Roman architecture. Furthermore we visited the Arena, a Roman circular structure, an open theater for all kind of spectacles. It is smaller than the Colosseum in Rome, but well preserved and still used for sport events. It gave us a good idea of Roman will to build and of Rome's power as revealed in architectural vision and proportions. There are other vestiges of Roman architecture in Nîmes, as well as the beautiful LaFontaine gardens, dating from the 17th and 18th centuries, where on a marble bench we had our egg lunch, and where for a while we forgot our multiple troubles. It was warm, children were playing around us; the park, extraordinarily attractive in its French geometric design.

We went for a walk and then sat down in a little coffee shop on the Avenue Victor Hugo and ordered coffee and cake. The coffee, of course, was no coffee, and the cake was some kind of concoction which some marmalade held hardly together. It was like a symbol for the whole make believe we staged with this outing to Nîmes.

There was in Vienna at the beginning of this century a philosopher by the name of Hans Vaihinger. Vaihinger condensed this theory in a book entitled "Die Philosophie des Als-ob" (The Philosophy of the AS-IF) and he explained that in life as in science we cannot do without a fictitious premise, posing "as if" it were true; the most valuable insights—according to Vaihinger—can be gained by this process.

Here we were in Nîmes, as if we were tourists, had coffee and cake, as if it were coffee and cake, walked on the streets and admired ancient beautiful buildings, as if we didn't have a worry in the world. And nobody would believe it: it worked for a whole Sunday. Vaihinger's theory worked very well for us.

The next month—it was now October 1942—we learned that Pablo Casals, the world renowned cellist, would give a concert in Montpellier, and we had an irresistible desire to hear him. First of all we wanted to listen to this great musician, and then we wanted to see the courageous man who had vowed never to return to his beloved homeland Spain as long as Franco's Fascist night was spread over it. I did not want to take any chances, went to the Police and got a safe-conduct to go to Montpellier (25 km West of Lunel) for the day of the Concert; and we went. The Hall was filled to the last seat. There was no electricity, only candles. The stage had a dozen candles around the piano and the music stand for Casals. It became clear from the beginning that this was much more than a Concert. This was an affirmation of the human spirit, a gauntlet thrown to the inhuman backsliding and oppression. A small unquenchable light burned, surrounded by impenetrable darkness. When he, Casals, came out on stage, everybody in the hall rose, all of us united in the thought that Evil has but a time and would be defeated.

Casals was a man in his fifties, short, balding—we saluted him, so to speak, and we honored him for the spirit he stood for. Then he began to play. The program contained the Chaconne by J. S. Bach, transcribed from violin to cello, a Beethoven Sonata and an Albeniz. No Mendelssohn and no "Shlomo" by Ernest Bloch (which he plays so masterfully). Jewish composers were forbidden by Hitler and his gang.

We listened to this great musician, we listened to every tone because there was so much more to it than melodies and movement. There was a language that told us loud and understandably: Do not despair, do not give up as we, preceding generations, never gave up. Fight for your survival the best way you can. The main thing is to stay alive—as a partisan in the Russian woods, as a hungry stateless man under police surveillance, as a persecuted Jew in hiding, whatever your style and your choice and your opportunity, stay alive. "Into the storm and through the storm," as Churchill said. And if you stay alive, you will see the day when you can cry out: there *is* beauty in the world, there *is* truth and there *is* freedom.

Unfortunately we had to leave before the concert was over and we slipped out of the hall as quietly as we could. The last train was a quarter to eleven, and we had to run all the way to the station.

It had been now a year and a half since I had come to Lunel. The War was dragging on. From German victories in the beginning, there was now a stalemate. Our prayer was that this might be a turning point to the utter defeat of Hitler and his cohorts. Our lives and the lives of many millions depended on it. The marvelous and meaningful Casals Concert in Montpellier was the last reaching out towards and a reminder of a culture we had been reared in. From now on, late in 1942, a number of blows and dangerous setbacks came down on our heads, more and more threatening and accelerating during the last two years of the War.

9

A FEW DAYS after the Casals Concert I had a card from the Prefect telling me that I was *invited* (so the formula went) to come to the Concentration Camp of Agde during the morning hours of such and such a day in October, in order to be interned. Just like that. Out of the clear blue sky! A Camp in 1942 was something else than a Camp in 1940. In 1940 it had been a Labor Camp with more or less labor, but your life was safe. Now they could do with you whatever they wanted: they deported you to an unknown destination (and destiny), you just disappeared.

There had been rumors that Laval had to promise the Germans the concentration of all the foreign Jews in the unoccupied zone, and this politician without conscience or scruples had accepted the order without hesitation. What should I do? Hide somewhere? They would get Sonia. To prepare a hiding place in one or two days for the two of us was impossible.

"You know what, my dear, let us go for a walk and think this thing over," I suggested.

And we went through the narrow backstreets, not to be seen by anybody because Sonia could not hold back her tears. Suddenly —none of us had seen her approach—we found ourselves face to face with a lady who greeted us and stopped us. She seemed to know Sonia. Sonia introduced me:

"This is my husband, Mrs. Toureille."

"Glad to meet you, Mr. Barosin. But why are you crying?" And Sonia told her the whole story about the new danger of incarceration. Mrs. Toureille listened carefully and said:

"Mr. Barosin, please come over to see my husband this afternoon. If my memory is correct, he knows somebody in the office of that camp in Agde, a man who might be helpful." She gave me her address. I shook her hand and thanked her:

"Is 3 PM not too early?"

"No, that will be fine."

After she had left us, I asked Sonia who this Mrs. Toureille was and how and where she had met her.

"Mrs. Toureille is the wife of a Minister. I once stood in line in the big Market Hall here in Lunel where they sold eels; each would get two eels. When it was my turn, there were just two eels left. As a foreigner I felt embarrassed to take those two eels from French mouths because behind me the line was still pretty long. So I turned around and shared my two eels with the woman that stood behind me. It was Mrs. Toureille. She was very touched by my gesture and, whenever we meet on the street, she talks to me."

At 3 o'clock I was at Pastor Toureille's office. He was a man of about 5 feet 8 inches like me, middle aged, friendly, with a quick grasp in his eyes. I told him my story and the new predicament I was in.

"I intervened a few times in Agde," he said, "and so far I was successful twice. That is to say, they did not keep the men. But that was early this year. You know there is an aggravation for foreign Israelites" (a polite Frenchman does not call us Jews, but Israelites). "Here is what I will do. I will write to Mr. Baumann, an Office worker there, a letter on your behalf; you go and bring him this letter from me, and we will pray and see. Please write your full name on this piece of paper."

I did and got up.

"May I add my own prayers to yours," I said as I got up to leave.

"By all means," he smiled, "but no, sit down, I shall write this letter right away."

He did not seal the envelope, but handed it to me five minutes later. I thanked him, took his two hands in mine and left after asking him to remember me to Mrs. Toureille.

The day arrived in sorrow and deep anxiety. I put socks, a shirt, an aluminum pot, and other concentration camp prerequisites into my shoulder bag—the old music all over again—and rushed to the Railroad Station. Sonia could not hold back her tears.

"Darling", I said, "I have a strange feeling that I will be home tonight; but if not tonight, in a few days. You, during these days, stay more in Mrs. Manse's house (the neighbor) than at Mrs. Germain's. She understands the situation better and can hide you if it is needed."

I kissed her and jumped aboard the train to Agde to be interned. I was desperate. Were we already in the tentacles of the monster? Is this the beginning of the end for us? Is my final road: Agde, Drancy, Poland? I broke out in a cold sweat. My God, why are You torturing us and abandoning us?

The ride on the train took three and a half hours. Being an incorrigible optimist, I asked at the Agde Station when there would be a train back to Lunel. Five o'clock, I was told. From the Station to the vast concentration camp it was half an hour walking, and when I arrived at the office, it was a quarter to twelve. That was very bad timing. People are hungry at that time, are impatient and put work off to the afternoon. There were three desks; only two were occupied. Behind the one close to the door a young man was sitting: the receptionist. When I told him that I had a letter for Mr. Baumann, he pointed to the other table near the window, occupied by a middle-aged, bespectacled German Jew. I said:

"Good morning, Sir, I have a letter for you from Mr. Toureille", and I put my Prefecture postcard and the letter before him.

"Ah, good Pastor Toureille, how is he?"

"Oh, he is fine."

"Still in Lunel?" he inquired.

"Yes, he is."

Then he began to read Toureille's letter. Suddenly he looked intently at my face.

"Barosin? Are you in any way related to L.H. Barosin?"

"He is my father."

"Now this is unbelievable." He got up from his seat. "L.H. is one of my best business friends. I work in Plywood too, you know. Where is your father now?"

"He got to the United States some time ago."

"We had many business deals together. Now isn't that something? What are you doing, Jack?" He looked at the letter.

"Right now I am not doing much, except waiting to be sent back to Lunel from this Camp." He gave me a good belly laugh.

"Well, let me think of something, Jack. I will certainly do everything I can to liberate the son of one of my best friends. And you have quite a father, you know; honest through and through. Now, seeing you in close up, you look very much like him. Wait a second, I will bring you something to eat, and then we will get busy. It may take a few hours. Sit down right here and wait for me."

He left the room. My heart was pounding. I turned to the young man at the other desk.

"May I smoke in this room?"

"You may, go ahead."

I waited for about eight minutes. Mr. Baumann reappeared with a big soup bowl full to the rim, a good piece of bread and a little piece of "Cheese"; in the soup I saw a good piece of meat swimming around. I thanked him very much for his kindness. He took from his drawer a few sheets of paper and told the young man to fill in all my identity information, and then he left.

I took my lunch over to the receptionist's desk and, while eating, I gave him my identity, pretty detailed even. It took quite a while until he was through. The door opened. A huge, fat Frenchman whose face looked like that of Louis XIV came in. I was met by a pair of pendulous jowls, two mean eyes and an unending nose. The young man jumped up; so did I.

"Who is he?" He honored me with a split second look.

"A new man to be incorporated, Sir." He looked at the papers the young man had written out.

"Hmm." Out he went, no questions asked.

"This was the Commandant", said the young man. "You see, you first have to be incorporated, and then we can detach you, say to agricultural work in . . ."

"Lunel", I helped.

"Lunel, that's right. Do you know some Frenchman who could employ you?"

"Yes, Mr. Dussel in St. Just."

"Perfect".

At about 1:30 Mr. Baumann returned, smiling, picking up the papers that his assistant handed him.

"The Camp doctor has to examine you, but he cannot make it before three o'clock. In the meantime would you please go into the next room, Jack, I have some work to do."

"Of course, and again many thanks for the delicious lunch."

At five o'clock was my train. If the doctor was late, I would hardly make it. I had half an hour to walk to the Station. But how could I tell Mr. Baumann that I wanted to make the five o'clock train. Of course, I could not. I should thank God for the miracle He had performed here before my eyes, sending me an angel in the person of a good friend of my father's who would return me to freedom. I should not make ridiculous demands. But was there a later train? Doubtful. So I would walk around, have a look at this medieval city, call Sonia, give her the good news and tell her that I would be home tomorrow. There were certainly hotels in Agde.

It's a quarter to three. Ah, if the doctor were a fine chap, he would come right now. The door opens. It's Mr. Baumann. We both sit down on the bench.

"Tell me a bit about you, Jack." Baumann seems to have all the time in the world . . . "You are married, aren't you? Yes, your father told me. You know, I lived in Frankfurt . . ." and he veered off into part of his life story which was of average interest.

While he lit a cigarette, I looked at my watch: Three fifteen. The door opened and the doctor came in. Baumann left us alone. Quickly I took off my shirt and he examined me. He took all his time, made notes on a piece of paper, and finally he gave me a small glass and said:

"The first door in the corridor: I need some urine."

I rushed over to the toilet, but I could not do it. I talked nicely to my body:

"Please do it for me, the train won't wait" . . . Nothing happened. I went back to the doctor and told him that I could not urinate right now. Could he continue the medical examination without the urine? No, he has to have my urine, he has to make an analysis.

"But take your time, don't be nervous. We have plenty of time," and he sent me back. Time was just what I did not have, but how could I tell him? So I went back. Nothing doing. Isn't that ridiculous; a big man depending on the good will of . . . It took five more minutes of persuasion, until I could bring the doctor what he wanted. He said he would analyze it right away and left the room. Four o'clock. I lit another cigarette. At four fifteen he was back.

"Alright, we can write out the discharge papers now." He returned to the young man in the Office. After he left, I took the young assistant aside and told him that I would appreciate it very much—I offered him my pack of cigarettes—if he could write out the papers as quickly as possible. My train would leave at 5 PM.

"Oh, I wonder whether you will be able to make it. It is four twenty-five now. But all right: I will try my best."

It was four forty when I had it signed; he handed me a copy. I thanked Mr. Baumann and the young man and wished them all the luck in the world. Until the big gate I walked normally, wasting precious time (who knows, Louis XIV may show up again in the last minute and ask silly questions), but then I started to run as I have never run before, and I ran and ran all the way to the station. I arrived at four fifty-nine, the train was standing there and waiting for me, and when I jumped on it, it just started to move.

I sat there in my compartment, getting my breath back after I had quieted down, and I recapitulated the whole miracle. It happened in four stages. First, the eel purchase and Sonia's splendid idea to share the eels with the next lady who was Mrs. Toureille. Second step: The unexpected meeting of Mrs. Toureille in a deserted back alley the day before I had to go to Agde. Third step: the letter of Pastor Toureille to Mr. Baumann, and the fourth step: Mr. Baumann in Agde turned out to be a good friend of my father's and decided right away to do everything in his power to let me go.

If you write a movie script, beware of too many coincidences and improbable incidents; nobody would believe your story, but would say that this could happen only in a poorly thought out movie, never in real life. But this is the stuff miracles are made of, logical, coherent all the way through. And I had the joyful understanding that the four "acts" had a common denominator: they were based on actions of decency and goodness.

I arrived in Lunel at eight thirty and fifteen minutes later I turned the key in the door. Sonia had watched at the window and rushed out to meet me.

The next day we went to thank the Toureille's and to tell them the whole story in four chapters; Pastor Toureille with an increasingly serious expression on his face listened to me. The more I spoke, the wider his eyes opened.

"God has hidden you in the shadow of his Hand."

Illustrations by Jacob Barosin

Job by Jacob Barosin

"Are you Mr. Barosin?" Arrest in Paris.

Prisoners waiting in the Buffalo Stadium in Paris.

Foreign laborers in Langlade steal a piling for firewood from a dead end
train tressle during the cold winter.

It was bitterly cold in barrack H 9 of the Gurs concentration camp.

Names called for deportation. Every ten days 1,000 people were deported
to an unknown destination (most died in Auschwitz).

After the weekly deportations, women came from their quarters to see if their husbands were still there.

A view from inside the Gurs concentration camp.

A meeting with Mrs. Toureille.

Jacob and Sonia Barosin reading the Bible in Montmejean while hiding in a room where they could only whisper and could not walk during the day so the children in class downstairs would not hear them.

The room in the Montmejean schoolhouse where the author and his wife hid. Chestnuts and other food were kept in a briefcase so that mice would not reach them.

Two policemen approach Montmejean.

Attending a candlelight concert by Pablo Cassals in Montpellier.

With Boris, bargaining with Scholastique for black market goods.

A Breughel-like peasant dance at the farewell party held for the Barosins.

An effigy of Hitler, hanging after the German retreat.

"Free again." The author and his wife in their Paris apartment, August 1944.

Jacob Barosin and Natalie Barosin in Paris, 1981.

10

ON THE 8TH of November 1942 we heard on the Radio that a great British Army had started an offensive in North Africa and that the resistance of Rommel's Africa Corps was broken. With the beginning of this Allied victory the face of the War had changed. So had our lives. War and disaster had come closer and closer to us.

We lived in a ground floor room the windows of which faced the street. Three days after the start of the British offensive in North Africa we were awakened early in the morning by a song that had been one of the marching songs I had been taught in my childhood in Berlin.

"In der Heimat, in der Heimat, da gibt's ein Wiederseh'n"
"In the homeland, in the homeland, there we will meet again"

And it was not sung by quick marching, nervous French soldiers, but by slow moving, heavy boots, many of them. I ran to the window. Here they were with their square helmets, German soldiers, occupying the whole of France, marching through the streets of until now peaceful, dreamy Lunel. After the BBC news it had to be expected; but to be talked about and *promised* is one thing, to see it happen before your eyes, to face the catastrophe, something else entirely.

One fact became obvious: We could not stay on in Lunel, we again had to run away. But to where? The whole of the French territory was being occupied. Where would we get the right to stay, even under surveillance? A hundred thoughts chased each other while I got into my clothes. To go to Nice is out of the question, to go to Paris, too. A mountainous region might be better than the flat land around Lunel. A chance to hide would be greater. After all, they could not occupy every little mountain hamlet.

A quick breakfast, and I hurried over to the Police captain, a very friendly and decent man.

"You are still here, Mr. Barosin?" he asked me astonished.

"Yes, but I want to get out. Could you give me and my wife a safe-conduct?"

"Where to?" It was obvious he wanted to be helpful.

"I don't know, any suggestion, Sir?"

He looked at the map of France and pointed with his pencil to a few places:

"There is Rodez, there is Marvejols, Florac. . . ."

I had heard of Rodez, not Marvejols. Florac sounded nice, floral, flowers . . .

"Are there mountains in Florac?" I asked.

"They are all over," he smiled at my ignorance of French geography.

"So Florac it will be with your permission," I decided. He wrote out two long sheets of paper according to our identity cards and handed them to me.

"When do you intend to leave?"

"Tomorrow or the day thereafter," I said.

"The sooner the better; we are expecting some nasty new administrative measures to be taken against foreigners. I am sure you understand what I mean." I looked into his eyes.

"I do."

"Good luck, Mr. Barosin."

We shook hands as friends. From the Police precinct I rushed to the Railroad Station to find out how to get to Florac and when the train would leave Lunel. My train, the next morning, would be at 7 AM; with two changes of train I would be in Florac at about 11 AM. Then I ran home to tell Sonia about the quick action that was necessary. I would go first, alone, to look for a room or a small apartment in Florac. Then I would come back to Lunel for Sonia. The words of the Police Captain were ringing in my ears: "You are still here?" and "the nasty administrative measures." Sonia and I understood only too well.

I went to Eugene and Augustine to tell them that we would be leaving for good within the few days. They were stunned, but they guessed that we were doing the right thing. They were sad; so was I because we had become real good friends. He was a fine chap, Eugene.

Sonia and I had been packing our suitcases so often in recent years. What do we do with the preserves? I put most of them into a wooden box Mrs. Germain had given me. Who knows how the food situation in Florac will be? Florac has two thousand inhabitants and is the second city in the Lozère Department. The other *big* city (with 6,000 inhabitants) is Mende, the seat of the Prefecture.

I took a full suitcase and the big box with the preserves to leave them in Florac or wherever I would find new living quarters. After Uzès, which was coal mining country, the landscape became beautiful. But all kinds of thoughts were running through my poor head, hurting each other in their speed. My mind was not able to take in the beauty of the countryside, not at this point.

Was this the right road we were taking? It was all guesswork. How did I know that the "nasty administrative measures" had not yet reached the Department of Lozère? And if they have, what kind of Police Captain would I find in the Precinct? Would there be a gendarme right away at the station to arrest me then and there or would the Police Captain be helpful and friendly as the Lunel man had been? After all, all I have is a safe-conduct to get to Florac, i.e. not to be arrested on the train. I had no residence right in Florac.

When, approaching Florac, that little country train swung a turn over those precipices on narrow wooden bridges, I did not see the spectacular beauty of the Cevennes mountains, and I prayed that we would not land too suddenly down there, but would get to Florac in one piece. Finally I arrived in this attractive little tourist city which had not seen money spending tourists for quite some time, and the Railroad employee who took my luggage on deposit, correctly did not take me for one.

First I walked the streets up and down for a sign *Room for rent*. There was none. So if there is nothing in the *big* city of two thousand, let's look for a smaller place near Florac. Ispagnac sounded Spanish and intriguing. It was situated three miles from Florac, surrounded by mountains. Maybe it was even more appropriate in case it was necessary to hide. Let's go. It was pretty cold, though the sun had come out. I walked at a brisk pace and made it in an hour to Ispagnac, which was a rather large village, not a town, very ancient, with narrow, crooked, climbing streets and few people outside. I asked a few women and rang a few doorbells. There was nothing but mistrust and negative answers. So Ispagnac I had seen and I decided that it was not the place for us to be. Back on the road to Florac. While walking I ate the sandwich that Sonia had prepared.

The Cevennes country (called so after the Cevennes mountains) had a long history of heroic resistance against invading troops, even when these invading troops were French troops sent by His Catholic Majesty the King to subdue Protestant strongholds in these mountains. Those were bloody religious wars, and this region had kept its strong will to resist outside interference; they rejected those laws, made by their central government, laws from outside that would not fit their own ideas of freedom and self-reliance. I mention these historic facts so that the story that happened to me now during the next two hours could be understood in the context of this Cevennes Country past.

When I re-entered Florac, I felt a little tired. Not so much physically, but I had hoped like in Caesar's "Veni-vidi-vici" (I came —I saw—I conquered) tempo to find something appropriate in one day; but I saw that shortly I would have to call Sonia to tell her that I would have to stay overnight in Florac and try my luck for a room tomorrow. So here I was slowly wandering down the Avenue Monestier which is Florac's main artery, when I stopped before a beautiful villa with a tastefully landscaped lawn and garden in front, protected by a high wooden fence. I stood there for a while, knowing that I was losing my time because there was nothing here to look for in my search for a room, when suddenly I saw a gentleman (he must have seen me from behind one of his tall bushes) coming straight up towards me. He was tall, handsome, graying, well dressed, with high riding boots, the perfect country gentleman. He opened the door and came out, while I was remaining on the street.

"Bonjour, Monsieur, you are looking for something or somebody?" he smiled.

"Yes and no. I am a foreigner in Florac and I am looking for a room for me and my wife. My wife would follow me from Lunel where we have been living until now; but evidently there are no rooms for rent in such a beautiful villa as yours. I apologize."

"Are you Jewish, Monsieur?"

Bang. This man was a Vichy agent, a Laval lover, and he would turn me into the Gendarmery which I had just passed.

"I must confess, Monsieur," I began cautiously, "that before the Germans came to occupy this good country of France, I have never heard questions like this. Yes, Sir, I am a Jew."

"I apologize for the bluntness of my question, young man, and I hasten to add that we here in the Cevennes and in Florac are well disposed towards the Jews; we try to help them as much as we can. I say this not only to put you at ease, but to let you know how ashamed I am about what happens presently to your coreligionists in my country."

"My name is Jacob Barosin." Now *I* smiled.

"My name is Ernest Audrix." We shook hands. "As to your question about renting a room, no, we dont sublet a room here, where I live with my wife and one of our daughters who has her little girl, Françoise, with her. By the way, do you have children?"

"No, unfortunately not".

"I have a small two-room apartment, nicely furnished, in one of my apartment buildings in Florac. If you want to have a look at it, I will bring the keys, put on my coat and walk right over with you".

"I thank you very much, Monsieur Audrix."

While he disappeared in his house, I stood there, tears coming to my eyes, and my heart was beating an "allegro agitato."

The apartment was on the third floor of a nicely kept old house on Main Street. A watchmaker's shop was on the ground floor. We walked up the old wooden staircase, and he opened the door. Splendid. A fireplace room, where the cooking was done and a long bedroom with a window to the street, a chest, a wardrobe, wash bowl and a bed with mattresses and down blankets that looked four feet high. He saw on my face that I was very pleased with it.

"How much, Monsieur, would the monthly rent be?"

"Would frs. 150 a month not be too much?" he asked hesitatingly. He wanted to give me a break, to help me somehow, that was clear.

"Oh no, that's not enough, Sir. I pay frs. 200 for one room in Lunel right now."

"Alright, alright make it frs. 200 then. By the way, the toilet is on the second floor; you have to go down one flight. I will show you."

Then he took me to his home where I was introduced to his wife, Lucie Audrix, a still pretty woman in her late fifties, lively in her movements and with laughing eyes that changed their expression quickly. I was invited to a cup of coffee. The villa was vast, had two large living rooms (what the French call *Salon*) and furniture of such a delicate taste as I had seldom seen in a private home. Each piece of furniture, down to the small foot stool, was an antique and a piece of art at that, dating back to the 18th century. I do not know enough about French furniture, but I could make them some believable compliments about their exquisite taste, throwing in a bit of historic names and technical jargon on furniture styles, so they understood right away that they talked to a farmhand who had tried his hand at other tasks before the war.

We signed a little paper and I left them, certain that I would find in Mr. and Mrs. Audrix not only good landlords, but friends and protectors if need be.

It was 5:30 PM. The train would leave Florac at 8. But since I would have a long wait in Ste. Cecile d'Andorre and two hours wait in Nîmes, I would arrive in Lunel at 3:20 in the morning.

I felt in my pocket the precious key to our new apartment. From the Railroad station I brought my suitcase and the box with the preserves right up the three flights, and then I treated myself to a hot soup in the small hotel-restaurant.

I was sorry to wake up my wife before 4 AM, but I had so many good news about my successful trip to Florac, about the fine people I had met and about the convenient apartment I had rented.

"I will get our things together and in a few days we will leave Lunel."

"In a few days?" she said. "No, right away."

"Why the hurry?"

"Because while you were away yesterday, a gendarme came to arrest you."

"To arrest me? But the Police Captain gave me a safe-conduct, he knew where I went."

"The gendarme told me that they had just received new instructions from Vichy via Montpellier. Maybe there is a higher up our Police Captain has on his nose."

"Aha, the nasty new administrative measures, to arrest and torment Jews, he had talked about. Alright then, let's pack the rest and get out here with the 3 PM train."

We had an early breakfast and began packing. We insisted with Mrs. Germain to tell anybody who wanted to see us, especially gendarmes and Police officers, that we were not at home. Poor woman, all this deadly hide-and-seek game was so new and incomprehensible to her, that I had to tell her three times to make sure that it would sink in. When the remaining two suitcases were ready, I ran over to Eugene and asked him to bring them on his tricycle to the Station. We went to say goodbye to a few people we had come to know, had lunch with Augustine and Eugene, and were at the station a quarter to three. There were no policemen for us. Everything went smoothly.

Under normal circumstances this would have been a pleasant trip through beautiful country, but this excursion into the unknown was a frightening undertaking. Dark had fallen before 5 PM, the lights in the train were dim, so was our mood. The wooden benches were hard.

We arrived in Florac around 9 PM. The streets were empty and filled with darkness. Fortunately *our* house was only a five minute walk. I was so happy when Sonia showed her delight about our new lodgings with a big kiss.

"Everything will be all right here in Florac, you will see," I tried to reassure her. "Tomorrow we will visit Mr. and Mrs. Audrix. They will be very happy to know you, I am certain of that and you may have a friend in Simone, their daughter."

The next day was a Sunday. Not knowing whether they were Church goers, we made our visit there in the afternoon. Sonia hit it off very well with them; right away there was a contact and even warmth.

We met Simone, a young divorced woman our age, maybe a year or two younger, and her little girl Françoise, who was friendly and lively. Mr. Audrix, an engineer, had gone into industry in his younger years, and his contacts in industry as well as in the financial world must have enabled him to amass a pretty fortune. The few names he threw around during our conversation like Deutsch-La-Meurte and others were meant to give me the right idea about the man I was talking to. He came from a solid French Dordogne farmer's stock, but it became clear in our conversation that there was no love lost for the Vichy Government, that we were on the same side of the fence, facing the same enemy. At one point, wanting to reassure me of his pro-Jewish feelings or to give a sample of his philosophy in life, he said:

"You see, Mr. Barosin, I have great friends among your people. I can say that I made my fortune thanks to them, and it is my conviction that the old saying is right: 'Don't eat of the Jews and don't eat of the Pope. If you do, you are lost.'"

"I could not agree more with you," I answered. "However before being smashed, Hitler will have eaten a lot of Jews."

"We here in Florac, as I told you before, do everything we can to help. Mrs. Lapierre and her husband, a high school teacher, are very active in aiding refugees. I think there are 28 Jewish men, women and children here, some of them without any means. We, the Lapierre's, Pastor Gall together with the Jewish Assistance Organization in Marseille do everything possible to find shelter for them, to feed and protect them. The Mayor of Florac, a Medical man, Dr. Maury, has a good relationship with the Under-Prefect here. Should those nasty administrative measures you are talking about ever come to be imposed in our region, Dr. Maury will be the first to be advised, and these poor threatened people will immediately be hidden away."

I had tears in my eyes. I could not help it. I got up and kissed him on both cheeks. He was moved by my gesture.

"Now let's talk about something else. Where do you buy your meat in Florac?"

"Did you say 'meat?' We haven't seen meat for a long time."

"Alright: tomorrow at ten pick me up here. I will introduce you to our cousin Césarine who has a butcher shop around the corner. You'll get a good size steak there whenever you are hungry."

I thought he exaggerated. We did not believe our ears. But so it was. The next day Césarine, an aging roundish woman with a husband half her age, sold us a steak a foot long and a good inch thick, red and fresh and juicy. The baker sold us bread without tickets. What kind of paradise is this?

During the next few days after registering at the police, we took walks around Florac and the outlying villages. 2000 feet high mountains surround this town on all sides, as if to protect this little valley and its river, the Tarnon. Winter had definitely come and we tried to dress as warmly as we could. Mr. Audrix allowed us to take the wood that was cut and lying around near our apartment door. On the second floor lived the watchmaker, Mr. Clare, and his wife. I did not like this little fellow too much with his false smile and his eyes that were not trustworthy. I kept away from him after our daily "bonjour." Much later we learned that he was an informer for the Gendarmery.

Our food situation had improved to such an extent that we could hardly believe it. So had the news for us:

The Germans were stuck deep inside Russia, and they did not like those Russian sub-freezing temperatures at all; neither had Napoleon's Grande Armée in 1812. The Russians put up a stiff resistance around Stalingrad, and the Krauts did not like that either. We felt that this might be the turning point in Hitler's war; we hoped and prayed that it were so. The Anglo-American landing in North Africa had brought the German hopes of seizing the Suez Canal (and thus cutting the British Empire in half) to an end. Rommel's troops were in full retreat. The French Fleet in Toulon, afraid of being taken over by the Nazis, bravely scuttled itself in accordance with Darlan's promise given to the British at the time of the Armistice.

The Vichy Government, spiced with a few diehards, collaborators, anti-Semites and pure fascists had no meaningful significance for the French people, nor for the occupying power. The whole Southern so-called *Free Zone* had been taken over by them. One day, on Main Street, I saw a fat civilian with a square skull, bespectacled, slowly walking and sniffing our good Florac air; for Jewish smells? I wondered and was frightened at the sight of this big, fat Gestapo man. Even to Florac they had come.

A few Resistance groups, unheard of until now, did appear here and there. But their activity was unimportant compared to the forces they faced. The French masses did not rise, though they hated the Germans as we did.

This was one of the most bitter reproaches we had for the Germans: They taught us to hate. I never in my whole life thought that I would be able to harbor such a feeling. These Krauts had become our deadliest enemies; they intended to and went about killing us all, each of us. The only weapon we had was our by now deep rooted hatred against those evil people, and the indomitable will to survive. So help us God.

We had to sit tight on the little money we had because there was nothing I could do in Florac to make a few francs. Christmas

(1942) was around the corner. The days passed quickly; three weeks had passed by since we had arrived in Florac. It was a great improvement over Lunel in every respect.

Walking one day with Simone, we were introduced to Mr. and Mrs. Lapierre who gave shelter and help to many of ours. What wonderful people. If their activity against the anti-Semitic Nuremberg laws (adopted by Vichy) became known, they would go the same way as those they protected.

We wrote to Paulette and Boris and gave them Mr. Audrix's address, so they would know where to write if something happened. There was no answer yet. Hopefully they are alright. Boris was a little bold and not careful enough.

Jacques, I heard, was hiding in the Lyon region (where his wife had come from) and played shepherd there. Jeanne being Catholic could stay on in Paris and keep the business going.

11

THE YEAR 1943 had arrived. Almost three and a half years of war now. How much longer could it last? How much longer could we last? Was there enough strength and will left in us to fight on and to survive this terrible situation? Would the Americans and the British ever land in Europe as they promised and as the Russians urged them to do? Young Frenchmen now were sent by the thousands, mostly forcibly, to work in German factories and to replace the Germans. Jews by the tens of thousands were being deported to the East from Drancy and many other concentration camps. We tried not to believe the rumors according to which they just killed our people. Did they starve them? We did not really know at that time, as we had never heard the word "Auschwitz". There were suggestions given to us from London to go into hiding whenever and wherever we could. Where could we go? How long could we stay in hiding? The Lapierres were worried, but Dr. Maury, the Mayor, had repeatedly assured Ernest Audrix that he would protect us, and that they would not get one Jew in his city. We wanted so much to believe him.

It seemed that Laval in his dealings with the Germans gave in on points where his conscience (if he had one) did not bother him: the *volunteers* for Germany and the Jews to disappear. Even some French Jews—until now protected by Pétain as French citizens —were being rounded up. With his horsetrading tactics Laval wanted to get some kind of independence for the Vichy Government, and to be more listened to by the German Ambassador in Paris, Otto Abetz.

Clare, the watchmaker, told me the other day, with a twinkle in his eye, that if I had some gold or silver or precious stones, he could get me a lot of money and of other things ordinarily unavailable. I answered him that not only did I—unfortunately—not have precious stones or gold, but that in my whole life I had never done any merchant's business, certainly not on the black market. From my shortlived military career I had a khaki shirt left to which he would be most welcome—with my compliments—if the collar was not too wide for him. His smile disappeared. He "knew" that all Jews had gold. He was a dangerous fellow. Did he want to trap me?

There was an elderly couple in Florac that had come from Paris to spend the War years there. Mr. and Mrs. Raymond were very friendly with Ernest and Lucie Audrix, the local aristocracy, and played bridge together. In these two people there was still alive the ancient French habit of distrust for any foreigner. They looked down on everything not French, and possessed a good portion of anti-Semitism which was considered *bon ton* (the in-thing) in higher French society. Needless to say that there was no contact between us except for an occasional "Bonjour, Madame" or "Bonjour, Monsieur."

Simone, who did not like Mrs. Raymond too much, told her mother Lucie that Mrs. Raymond had advised her that it would not be in her best interest to be seen too often with *that little Jewess* (meaning Sonia). "She may be," she said, "a very attractive young woman and obviously of good standing, but under the present circumstances, the less we deal with Jews, socially or otherwise, the better." There were so many of those moneyed upper class people in France that disliked the Germans—as a matter of taste—but who rejected the Jews with an inborn hatred. This came from the darkest Middle Ages and an obstinate Church indoctrination. Does not the Mass call us *Judaei perfidi*?

I was glad Sonia liked her stay in Florac. It looked like a long vacation. God only knew how long it could last. We wanted so much to believe in Dr. Maury's word and promise.

But it did not last. Thank God we both stayed alive, though we finally had to go into hiding. Here is what happened in those three months.

On February 16—I will never forget this date—after lunch, I took my water color box, my drawing pad, a bottle of water, and we both went up the hill that overlooked Florac from the other side of the little river Tarnon. This mountain belonged to Mr. Audrix, and he had shown me once a pidgeon coop from where one had a splendid view over Florac. I wanted to make a water color there. We got settled on a kind of stone bench. Sonia had her needle work. It was chilly, but you could smell a bit of spring air not far away. We had the big mass of the Cosse mountain, dark blue and menacing on the other side of Florac, pushing up into the sky, and down there in the valley the peaceful town with its houses and little gardens enclosed by walls, alleys and narrow streets, a marvel of unplanned city building that was a delight to the eye.

I had one of my better days: the sketch came out well. I proceeded carefully—water colors are a delicate and difficult medium —but the colors seemed right and fresh. The mood of the overwhelming mass of the background mountains was just as it should be, and Florac with its little Church spire in the distance began to shape up. However I felt at a certain point that this was all I could do that day. There was a bit of fatigue after more than an hour of concentration, and I knew that I would make mistakes if I forced myself to go on and to finish it at that time. There were still areas of white paper left. I stopped right there and said to myself: I will finish it tomorrow afternoon. I let it dry, cleaned my paint box, packed our things and we descended the hill.

Sonia remembered that there was a distribution of live chickens, one to a family, twice a year, and that we were entitled to it now. She had the tickets in her pocket book, we might as well go and pick it up. It turned out to be a real good day: my work on the water color was coming along and we got a chicken which we would prepare for a royal feast with our new friends this weekend. The world was thrown into turmoil and into a murderous and barbaric war, the echoes of which came from a distance to us every day in Radio and press, but here was an exceptional day when we succeeded in our efforts to eliminate and to forget the nightmare for a few hours, when we had peace in our hearts.

The next morning, February 17, I went down to the back-yard to see if my chicken was still in the big box where I had put it and attached it with a string. There it was, running wild in its prison, not quite understanding what had happened to its freedom. I gave it some chicken feed and climbed back up the three flights, after filling a big container with water at the pump which was right in front of the house.

We had breakfast and made it a lazy morning. A little later, Sonia wanted to see Mrs. Lapierre, who was very friendly with her. I would go to see Mr. Audrix, but not before 11 o'clock. I opened my water color pad and looked at my water color. I may try a touch here and a highlight there. It looked so good to me, I could hardly wait for the right light in the early afternoon to finish it. Those joys are the artist's reward.

Suddenly we heard footsteps coming up the staircase, first distant, then closer and closer. They are on our landing now. We hold our breath. The bell rings. I put my finger on my lips to indicate to Sonia not to make a move; she is very pale. We are frozen. They ring the bell a second time. Total silence again. Then they make a few steps outside the door and begin to descend. When I heard their steps far down on the ground floor, I slowly opened the door. That was my undoing. The door squeaked a little. Our assumption that both gendarmes had left was wrong; one of them, the tricky one, had stayed on the second floor beneath us, and when he heard the squeaking door being opened, he came back up to our floor. He called back to his colleague who was about to leave the house. There are mistakes in life for which you may pay more dearly than for a crime. They gave me fifteen minutes to get dressed and to pack my suitcase. I took a frs. 1000 bill from our 4000 and put it into my shoe.

"Do you arrest women, too?"

"Ah non, Monsieur, Madame is free. As to you, we would ask you to follow us to the Gendarmery to answer a few questions."

I know the music by now. The main tune is: are you Jewish? Sonia accompanied me and the two gendarmes to the Gendarmery not far from Audrix's house. It was about 11 AM. There were two more Jews they had caught, Glass and Bauer. The day promised to be a *good* one for Jew hunting. They took our identity papers and began writing, writing. A man in civilian clothes approached us:

"I am Gabriel Thau from the so-and-so Jewish Organization in Marseille, and I have a little money to distribute among you. Each of you will receive frs. 1000. You just sign here," and he took the bills out of his pocket.

"I have never in my life taken 'nedoves'" (the Hebrew word for handouts), I objected, "and I will not start today." Thau looked at me incredulously, half admiringly.

And then we three were led into a narrow cell, the door was left open, so we could still see and talk to our wives (Glass's 15 year old daughter, in tears, was there too), cry with them, give them our last suggestions—to go into hiding immediately—stroke their heads and kiss them. The gendarmes were almost humane and observed us from a distance. Another two men were brought in, pale, bewildered. We were five now. At about 12 o'clock the ladies were asked to leave, and the door was shut, a heavy iron prison door with a very small window in the upper middle.

I sat on a cot trying to grasp what had happened. Two hours ago I had pumped water into my container, a perfectly free man then, and had observed the chicken that I had put into its prison yesterday. And now two hours later I was myself locked in. That heavy door was the limit of my world. I was again caught in a web from which there was no escape. What is that crazy door doing there? Why can I not go out? One of Raphael's Stanza's in Rome suddenly came to my mind: the angel freeing Peter from prison, all bathed in light. But here is much darkness, and no angel is in sight for us. I spent a sleepless night in that hole. This was the 17th of February.

On the 18th in the morning we were taken out at about 9 o'clock. Outside on the street there were Sonia and Mrs. Audrix. Our little group of about fifteen people and the four gendarmes accompanying us began marching in the middle of Avenue Monestier towards the Railroad Station. We, the five arrested men, would be shipped somewhere. One of the gendarmes took my suitcase to carry it for me. Mrs. Audrix, not afraid to march next to me, gave me a fountain pen and said:

"This is not a present, Jack. This you will return to me when you come home."

"With God's help," I answered and put it into my pocket.

"Sonia will probably stay with us for a little while," she whispered into my ear, and I pressed her hand against my heart.

It was 9:40 AM when, from the train window, I had a last glimpse of Sonia. She became smaller and smaller, and then she disappeared into some grayish crowd which itself became a disappearing spot.

"Where do you take us?"

"To Gurs."

For the first time in my life a thought crossed my mind: Would it not be better if the end came quickly and without any more suffering? How much can a man take? Almost four years of arrests and concentration camps, of running away and poverty, of dangers and threats to your life and to your loved ones. But immediately I rejected this death wish because it went basically and fundamentally against our ancient belief in the preciousness of life. Life had to be conserved and maintained under all circumstances.

We five men were each given half a bread and a small hard sausage for the day. It was chilly, and though the train was heated, I kept my winter coat on. I did not look out the window, but I sat there, with my hands in my pockets, and my eyes closed. I wanted to see nothing, to hear nothing, to forget where I was and where I was going.

So finally I was caught between the wheels of the horrible German machine. What would happen to Sonia? Since I could not protect her anymore, I was so glad that Lucie said that they would take her into their house. They liked her very much; but would she be safe there? My thoughts tried to cling to any aspect that seemed favorable. For instance: since we were going to Gurs which is in the Southwestern corner of France, I would probably not be taken to Germany right now. Maybe Gurs had just become another Labor Camp, where we would do some work? And once there, one could find a way to escape. The Spanish border was not very far, and the Spaniards do not send escapees back as the Swiss did in many instances. It was rumored that Franco, protecting the Jewish refugees, may really be a Marrano whose ancestors converted from Judaism under duress during the Spanish Inquisition.

After the Germans had suffered a tremendous defeat at Stalingrad—as we had heard the other day on BBC—the time should be near when the Americans and the British should finish the Germans off by establishing a second front for them. Maybe they will come in this summer of 1943. Will we, Sonia and I, be able to hold out that long? This is mid-February.

We had to change trains in Ste. Cecile and approached now Nîmes, a city which I knew so well. From here we took the Southern direction, a bit to the West, past Lunel, Montpellier and other towns. Passing Lunel I looked out the window for a moment, but since the train does not cross the town, but passes it by, there is nothing much to see. The train goes on. Another stop in my life vanishes into the fog of time.

Two of the gendarmes were nice fellows, almost apologetic. Two of our own men hardly spoke French. Glass was always wiping tears from his eyes and repeating that he would never see his wife and his child again. He said that he would never get out from behind barbed wires. All our attempts to change those lugubrious thoughts, to give him some hope, were unsuccessful. And who knows, maybe his premonitions were right.

Sète—Béziers—There is the Mediterranean again . . . Our last stop was Oloron; the train did not go any farther, this was the end of the line. My hope was that it would not be the end for me, as Glass was lamenting all the time. Darkness had fallen. It was eight o'clock in the evening. We had a cup of coffee at the Railroad Station while waiting to be taken by truck to the concentration camp. We arrived a little before ten at Gurs. It looked like a tremendous camp. A few people were in the Office building. The gendarmes delivered us to the office workers, got their papers signed, handed our identity papers over to the civilians and were shown to their sleeping quarters, where they would spend the night.

"Do you have any money?" I am asked.

"No," I lied.

"Open your suitcase." I did as I was told. He went through my things. "OK. Now your name, born where, when, nationality . . . You come from Germany?"

"Yes"—and under "nationality" he writes "German". I interrupted his writing:

"Though I came from Germany, I am not a German, but a Latvian." He looked up.

"You have any proof?"

"I don't have my Latvian passport, but I have a photocopy of my father's passport here," and I showed it to him. My father and I look very much alike. He crossed out "German" and wrote in "Latvian."

From what I could learn later, this saved my life because all German Jews—Glass included—were deported East.

They took us to the barracks and left us in one with about twenty beds and nobody there; they told us that since it was late, we would spend the night there and would be assigned to other barracks tomorrow. It was very cold. We did not undress, but fell on our matresses with our coats on and covered ourselves with the blankets we had received. I was so exhausted that I fell asleep within five minutes.

"All of you get up, coffee in ten minutes." A voice in the half dark morning greeted us. It was 6 o'clock. There was no toilet or washing facility. Somebody brought us a pot of "coffee" and half a bread. That made six slices for the five of us. We had our old cups or aluminum containers, and we took our breakfast in silence.

Gurs was a tremendous compound of barracks as far as the eye could see. Divided into twenty-five "isles" (isle is the French word for island) in alphabetical order, each isle letter had twenty numbered barracks. Three of us were taken to isle H and assigned to barrack 9 which already had fifteen inmates. Some were curious about the new arrivals and looked us over. Some took it in stride and did not even give us a glance. Almost all of them were Jews. Gurs, during the years, had undergone quite some changes. Built as a military barracks, Gurs had been filled with Spanish fighters in 1938/9 when Franco defeated them. Then in 1940 these moneyless and helpless men were sent to Labor Camps throughout France. (I had met some in Langlade.) They in turn made space for the refugees that streamed into France from the North at the time of the German offensive. At that time Sonia spent eighteen days there. Now, in 1943, it had become a camp from which Jews were being sent to Germany. For work or for what? we asked. Nobody could tell because no one ever came back.

In my barrack H 9 were men of all ages. I was given a bed, a cot really, between two friendly characters with whom one could talk. One was a man of 45 from Vienna and another, my age, a Polish Jew who had been a hairdresser in Belleville (Paris). Shmul Kurtzer had kept his military jacket as a souvenir of the short War in 1940, when he was in the French Army and had made his retreat to the Free Zone. He spoke a nice Yiddish, better than he spoke French, and his jokes brought some gaiety and laughter into an otherwise glum atmosphere. There were reasons for our despair. Every week a deportation was organized by the Administration, when about 1000 Jews, a full trainload, was sent to Germany. There were still approximately 5000 men, women and children left, and every day there were new arrivals from all over Southern France. Women and children were kept in the first five isles.

There had been a deportation two days ago. The next was scheduled for the end of the coming week. For the time being all German, Austrian and stateless Jews were being deported. Those who had any other nationality were not taken as of now because according to agreements between Germany and those countries the latter assumed "responsibility" for their Jewish nationals and dealt with them themselves according to their own anti-Jewish laws. For instance: no Rumanian had so far been deported from Gurs. This could change tomorrow.

We were served the same food I had become familiar with at Langlade; just a little more watery. As far as the population went, the same mix of good-hearted and mean, intelligent and stupid, civilized and uneducated, strong nerved and weak ones. All this with an admixture of suspicious fellows who always tried to drag you into a political conversation. Some of them did not look Jewish at all. Shmul told me right away to keep away from this one or that.

One barrack was transformed into a kind of Community Hall or social club. There was a piano. On Friday night and Saturday orthodox Jews would assemble a Minyan (ten men) and say their prayers. Did the Camp administration wish to lure us into believing that they had only good intentions, in order to avoid panic or rebellion? Or was it window dressing for inspection by Neutral commissions? They did not fool us. The fact is that Gurs was a waiting hall, an antechamber for gruesome things to come, that much we knew. And there were the constant and contradictory concentration camp rumors to enervate you, to frighten you and to sap your resistance. We were all half crazy, some were even more so.

There was in my barrack an old little man, sitting on his dirty bed and juggling with a few silver balls that he had manufactured himself with old aluminum foil. He was smiling all the time and trying to improve his skill. You would not guess at first glance that this little bespectacled unshaven man had been, a few years ago, a Professor of History at the famous Heidelberg University, a good Christian who went to Church on Sunday. But one of Hitler's gang found out that one of his grandmothers in the 19th century had been a Jewess; naturally he was automatically disqualified to teach History to "noble" Aryan youth. He was dismissed. Then the Germans, anxious to get rid of everything that had even a distant relationship with Judaism, expelled these unfortunate people. Concentration camps in the occupied territories seemed the adequate place for them. And this is how a few thousand of them were shipped from Germany to this distant camp of Gurs, this History professor and his wife (a full Aryan) among them. She had died last year and was buried on Camp grounds.

"Why do you do this juggling, Herr Professor?" I asked,

"It keeps me going," he smiled.

There is K.R., a businessman who had filled his life with buying and selling things. He just could not imagine life without making a monetary profit. It so happened that one of his classmates from Vienna worked at the office (a very privileged status among the internees because it was close to the power of the Commandant De Gruel—what a name). This man got him a permission to set up shop in our isle H, in an old, unused barrack. What did he sell? Writing pads, ink, postcards, radishes, turnips, cut logs, anything he could lay his hands on—through his good connections with office and kitchen. Business was good. If the next day he would be deported, his business would fall apart and he would not have the time to "sell" it. But he had the best occupation he could ever think of, he had his pockets full of money, and leave it to the boy to get it out. In our barbaric times you could buy a life for money.

A stove heats the barrack, insufficiently of course. Six men surround it to warm their blue fingers. Some of them have placed slices of turnip on top of this iron stove to toast them. It tasted awful, but it filled the stomach. Every slice had its place, and don't try to push another's slice a little further to squeeze yours into the center of heat. I have seen fistfights over turnip placements. Nerves were on edge; any pretext was good to get into a violent argument or a fight to let off steam.

The corner bed was taken by a frail old Polish Jew who prayed and read in his prayer book all day long. You could not see his eyes, only his lips were moving.

We were not in the German hell. Not yet. After all, this was France. But we were in limbo, a Kafkaesque state, from which some of us might be saved, and others could go really straight to that hell on earth.

What a surprise. Mrs. Sachs from Langlade showed up to get a few things which her husband had left in our isle; there was free access to the isles during the day. Poor Sachs had been deported last week. She came with her two children, the girl, eleven now, and a little boy, two and a half, born in Langlade or in Nîmes. She was very glad to see me, but sad that it had to be in Gurs. We talked about the "vacation" we had in the resort of Langlade. Would she be able to protect herself and the children much longer? I doubted it.

Gendarmes armed with rifles watched the camp from beyond the barbed wire fence. One came pretty close to have a look at what was going on inside an isle. I began a conversation with him:

"You look like a man one could talk to. Could I try?"

"Go ahead."

"What would happen if at night I made a hole under the fence and got away to the mountains?" I asked bluntly.

"I would not have seen anything because I am nearsighted in such cases. But five hundred yards from here there are militia men dug in — you cannot see them from here, and they would open up on you. Another five hundred yards mines would blow you apart. No, my poor man, you have to think of something better".

I thanked him and offered him a few "Celtique" cigarettes, the more expensive ones.

There was constant talk that maybe *tomorrow* a deportation would take place. From every barrack about ten men were to be taken, men from our isles and women and children from the others. It was always tomorrow or the day after tomorrow; and then nothing happened. But the day it really happened we were all frozen with fear. The isle exits were all occupied by militia and the barracks were locked after orders were given that everybody had to be fully dressed and to stand near his bed.

You are now in a locked prison cell. You wait. And then you hear the key turning in the lock, the door is opened wide. There they are: Two militia men, one plainclothes man. The militia man reads from a list the names of those who have to go. The men pick up their belongings, bags, suitcases — and leave the barrack. There is an undescribable tension in the room because everybody knows what *being called up* means. There is even a kind of compassion and seriousness on the faces of the militia men. One of them takes the suitcase of old Mr. Goldenberg, the praying grandfather, and carries it out for him . . .

Each time a name is called, and the man, silently, leaves the barrack, you ask yourself: will you be next? My heart beats hard. When it was all over for our barrack and they were ready to go to the next one, twelve of our men were outside, watched and counted by one of the armed militia men. The eight others who remained, including me, were saved from deportation. For this time, that is. Those who were taken were all German and Austrian Jews. They were ordered to march to the exit of the camp, where the trucks were waiting for them. I saw them becoming smaller and smaller on the muddy road until they disappeared. There was a deadly silence in the barrack. I sat down on my bed and tears were running down my cheeks, tears of rage about our defenselessness. For the first time I dreamed of a machine-gun. They were all good family men, husbands, fathers, grandfathers. Leibowitz the musician put his arm around my shoulder, and we cried together.

New arrivals filled the barrack. I was chosen headman to deal with the office. There was no work being done in Gurs. We were just lingering around, doing nothing and waiting for our name to be called. My new function gave me a kind of access to the office people. I heard from Grossmann that I have nothing to fear for the time being, because I am not a German or an Austrian citizen. Furthermore he told me confidentially that a man had arrived at the Prefecture in Pau—which administers the camp of Gurs—a French Colonel from Vichy by the name of Picard. Everybody knows that Picard is a Jewish name in France. He was trying hard to save certain foreign Jews from deportation. Jews who had married French girls and have French children. Or those who had done their military duty in France or who had shown in some way their good will and loyalty. There was a fight going on in Pau between him, backed by the French Military on one side, and the Laval people who, of course, did not give a dime for a Jew, but who wanted to please the Gestapo that had practically taken over. However Grossmann asked me to tell nobody about Picard because the whole thing may be swept under the carpet, and then he would be in trouble had the rumor spread.

After this good news, for two weeks there was no deportation. It was strange to see how quickly some of us took hold of a straw, if the word *hope* was written on it. Around the 12th of March, unexpectedly, all headmen of barracks were called to the office. We were told that there was another deportation planned for the near future, the date of which could not be divulged. We should prepare lists of family or other attachments of our men to France. Furthermore, we should get our military papers ready if we had such documents. One of the coming evenings we would be asked to submit these and other documents that might be helpful to officials who would come from Pau to decide on their validity and on our deportability.

I ran back to my barrack to bring my friends the good news about recognition of *French attachments* that might save them from deportation. Everybody wrote something on his piece of paper under his name. Nobody had a French wife, but some had children born in France. Four were prestataires as I had been, but this time, we had among us no real soldiers of the French Army as Shmuel Kuntzer had been. One, old Scheinfeld, had a French "aynikl", a grandson. There was not much to recommend them for office and Prefecture clemency and pity.

I had a card from Sonia. She said she was alright and that she would write as soon as she could. What did that mean: "As soon as she could?" The card came from Florac. That was reassuring.

A few days later—it must have been the 15th or the 16th of March (a month after my arrest) the headmen were again called to a certain barrack, late in the evening at 9 PM. When I arrived, there were at least fifty people in line, and the line hardly moved. It was very cold. After two hours I asked the man behind me to hold my place so I could get my blanket from my bed. Time was dragging on. Finally, a little after 1 o'clock in the morning I was let into the barrack.

Two rather young plainclothes policemen from Pau were sitting behind a long table with a lot of paper and with two of our office people.

"What's your name?"

"Jacob Barosin." He was looking for it in his papers.

"Ah yes, here it is. Have you served in the French Army?"

"I signed up as a volunteer in 1938. Here is my *call* ".

"Where did you see military action?"

"I did not because I was called up only in June of 1940. Here is my discharge paper from Marseille." I always kept a photocopy of it in my wallet. He looked at it and made a note behind my name. So here my discharge paper worked.

"You are a Latvian?"

"Yes, Sir." Another note behind my name.

"What about your men?"

"Joseph Scheinfeld has two French grandsons," he made a move with his hand as if he wanted to throw something into the waste basket.

"What else?"

"Leibowitz has two French born sons." He was looking for Leibowitz in his papers.

"But he does not have a French wife?" They knew everything.

"No, she is British. But he is a Rumanian citizen."

"Oh yes, I see." And he made a little note behind Leibowitz's name. Rumanians were not yet taken for deportation.

I tried whatever I could to save the men from deportation. Three of the others received an "honorable mention" from his pen. Did this young man realize that he might hold life or death in his hand? Was he aware of the fact that he could have saved innocent people? But then the Germans wanted their trainload of 1,000 Jewish men, women and children. The number was 1,000: and for this Frenchman from Pau who had to make his choice, those who were complete foreigners without attachment or proof of loyalty to France were the ones to be sacrificed.

I was out of the room. I was cold inside: I put my blanket again upon my shoulders. When I came to the barrack, everybody wanted to know how it went. I told them that I presented each case as well as I could, that he took some notes, that he looked sympathetically at our situation, but that he needs a thousand bodies for the Gestapo—and we are all in God's hands.

Two days later it happened. We were locked in as before, so nobody had a chance to escape. They left the five men and took away ten. The deportables had to wait half an hour outside. We five tried to smile to our comrades of misfortune. We encouraged them, spoke to them, told them that the world did not come to an end with Gurs, that they should never give up hope, and that they try for any opportunity to jump and to escape. But it might not have sounded convincing enough to them. I wished at that moment that every German should feel all his life what these men and we, the remnant, felt in this hour.

Then they left and disappeared on the horizon as all the others had done before them.

12

ON THE 21ST of March, Leibowitz and I were called to the office. We should prepare our things for tomorrow morning very early; we would leave Gurs with twenty other young men, and this was not a deportation.

"Where will we be sent? To Germany?"

"No, you stay in France, but we don't know where." Of course they knew. Will it be freedom or another of those camps? I did not sleep well that night. For almost five weeks I had been in Gurs now. Anyway, we should be grateful, especially to Colonel Picard who saved us this time. Tomorrow we would leave this terrible place that had seen so many tears.

It was 5 o'clock in the morning when they knocked at the door and screamed "Barosin and Leibowitz." We were on our feet, washed and dressed in no time. With our suitcases we made our way to the big Camp gate. There were twenty others taken from other barracks. Each one received a sausage and a whole bread; so, it is for a long trip. We were counted, our names were called, re-called and each of us passed through a narrow exit door to the outside of the Camp. It was 6:15 AM.

Three policemen in plainclothes accompanied us to the truck, and in half an hour we were in Oloron where the French Railroad begins at the French side of the Pyrenees. Once we were riding on the train I went over to the policeman and asked him where he was taking us. He said that it would be a Labor Camp in the Herault Department. I told him that I had lived in Lunel (Herault) for over a year. No, he said, where we were going would be farther West. It was a small town called Gignac. I took out my map of France, but I could not find it; it was too small.

"Is it under French Administration or does the Gestapo give the orders?"

"Oh no, this is a French Labor Camp where foreigners as you are fed and housed and do some agricultural work; of course," he added, "nowadays the Germans are never very far away. Are you from Germany?"

"No, I am a Latvian Jew."

"Oh, yes, I saw in the papers. You speak French remarkably well. Where did you learn it?"

"In school in Germany and then in France."

"How long have you been in our country?"

"Ten years now." Silence. Then all of a sudden he ventures: "As long as you stay in France, nothing bad will happen to you; but if I may give you an advice: Avoid being sent to Germany. By all means avoid it, and you understand what I mean by that." He looked into my eyes and then left me there.

We had to change trains, to wait at the Railroad Station for two hours and then board a local train that took us through all the villages in the region. At 4 PM we arrived in Gignac. The ending "ac" comes from the Latin "aqua", water; but we did not see any river, any water. It was all flat vineyard land.

In the office—quite a walk from the Station—our policemen handed our new guardians our identity papers; we were duly inscribed in the books, the three policemen waved us goodbye, and the twenty of us were taken to an old unused Church, where instead of pews and benches there were cots with matresses and two blankets waiting for us. We settled down, and those who had been there before us gave us some useful advice. They would take us to the fields; never work too hard. In no way attract any attention, not for good and not for bad. The old Army advice.

As in most of the concentration camps the office workers were themselves internees. They were nice fellows, especially the two Romano brothers who came from Salonika. Everybody seemed helpful, but everybody was frightened because recently German trucks had shown up in the fields where the work was to be done. The Krauts looked around and then left.

"When is Passover?" I asked my neighbor.

"Very late this year, on the 20th of April."

Dark had fallen. Two of our men brought in the usual evening soup. I was glad I still had a piece of bread and sausage which I shared with my neighbor. Then I hung my coat on a hanger on a line and lay down, covering myself with those blankets as well as I could. It was really getting cold in that Church.

At 7 o'clock next morning we got our breakfast: "coffee" and bread. Twenty minutes later the truck picked us up. We all climbed on it, standing shoulder to shoulder, as workers everywhere do when they are driven to work. It took about twenty minutes to get to the fields. We got off the truck, were given tools and a lot of onion roots which we had to plant a certain distance from each other. After two hours of constant bending, you felt your back. A cigarette was in order; the guards did not mind. My co-workers told me that within two days I would not feel my back anymore.

As soon as I was through with my day's work at 3 PM, I wrote a card to Sonia and gave her news about me, my whereabouts and my address. I had the feeling that my stay in Gignac would not be a very long one, but I preferred not to write anything about my feelings. The words of that policeman rang in my ears: "Avoid falling into German hands; avoid it by all means. You understand what I mean." That means that there comes a point when you would have to go into hiding, as Sonia must be in hiding by now. Even in a seemingly safe Labor Camp, the French in the near future would no longer be able to protect us. I did not like the sight of those Germans coming in their trucks and looking us over at work. I did not like it at all.

The War was going very badly for them. Except for Hitler, they knew by now that they could not win it. If the U.S. and England opened a second front this summer in France we might all be liberated by fall or early in winter. We learned that the Russians were back in the Ukraine and would soon assault German positions in Poland.

If I could find a hiding place with the help of our friends, for Sonia and for me, this would be the moment. It was now early in April 1943. This would be the last and most important step in our long odyssey. I had to sort out my thoughts and plan very carefully, because if we went into hiding, meaning into illegality, there was no way back from there; and in hiding we would have to wait for the end of the War, whenever that would be. Now all this would be all right in case France was liberated within six months. But what if it would take nine months, twelve months or even more than a year?

April 2. Fourteen years ago, my mother died at the age of fifty. I said my "Kaddish" for her (the Jewish prayer for the dead). Let her know that her son has not forgotten her in all his turmoil.

Again rumors ripped us apart. I met George Romano (the man from the Office) on the street and told him that I wanted to make a portrait sketch of him. He would pose the next day. Again we saw a German truck pretty close to our onion field. What were they doing there? I was getting scared and nervous.

George Romano is a fine and a very distinguished young chap; probably a descendant from the old Jewish Aristocracy in Spain. He liked the drawing very much. I did it in the office. They all seemed to like it. Now his brother wanted a sketch too. Of course, I would gladly do it.

Around the 15th of April there was a strange notice put up on the outside of the door of the Office building: Matzah would be distributed during the Holiday of Passover, but no travel permits were available beginning April 20. Knowing by now how devious the mind of concentration camp commanders and their Gestapo masters could be, I put two and two together: a deportation of all of us was brewing or a transfer or something. Theirs was typical simpleton thinking. They talked about Matzah to lure us into a trustful mood, but what they really wanted was to catch us all unaware, without any escape. There was no time to lose; I had to act quickly. I begged Romano for a travel permit. He said he couldn't give it to me.

"My wife is sick; I have to see her and the doctor." I would try to be back on the 20th; all I needed was a permit from the 17th to the 19th of April. He was a bit scared, but he finally gave it to me. I would not dare go on the train without valid travel papers; the trains underwent a heavy control these days. Romano's permit had the Company's stamp and he handed me my identity card, too, which was of the utmost importance.

We had for the last days worked in a field further out and had gotten our lunch soup in a small cafe-restaurant. The next day, at lunch time, I asked a friend to stand with his back against the telephone booth, so the guards could not see me inside. I quickly made a telephone call to Florac to Mr. Audrix, after having prepared all the necessary coins.

"Bonjour, Mr. Audrix, this is Jack Barosin."

"Bonjour, my dear friend, how are you?" He was very surprised.

"Oh, I am fine. How is everything with you and Mrs. Audrix?"

"Everything is just fine. Sonia has a little cold and must not go out for a few days."

"I see, Mr. Audrix. I am calling to tell you that I will be in Florac on the 18th or 19th of April and will be very happy to see you all."

"Oh, splendid. So will we. Take good care."

So Sonia was in hiding.

There was a train leaving Gignac in the direction of Nîmes at 7:30 in the evening. On the 17th at 6:30 my good friend and neighbor in the Church took my suitcase and my blue civilian coat to the station. I followed him at a distance in my working clothes — style foreign laborer. There were always spies in a Camp: furthermore, the guards might just have a walk or a drink in the Railroad cafe. But the air was clear. The station was deserted. It was almost 7 o'clock. My suitcase and my coat were left in the men's room. I quickly went in and locked the door.

I changed into civilian clothes and waited. What a long wait those twenty minutes were! Soon came the whistle of the train. When it stopped, I slowly moved towards it, opened the door and climbed up. With me there were two other people who boarded the train. And off I went — never to return to Gignac. Night had fallen.

The train arrived in the big city of Nîmes at 10 PM, just when the curfew had started. The train from Gignac had been a local train. Here in Nîmes I had to go to another station, for the Express train, and that station was on the other side of the city, about half an hour walk away. And curfew was on. How would I ever get there for the midnight train that would take me to Ste. Cecile, especially with that curfew over my head? There was nothing else to do but take a chance; dragging my suitcase, I started to walk through the dark. On the street there was not a soul. I had been walking about fifteen minutes when I saw in the distance a moving light coming towards me. The control officers! I threw myself flat against a housewall and groped my way slowly along until I found something like a door. It was not a door, but a doorway about six feet deep, enough to hide in. Would that the ground mercifully open up and swallow me. But it did not. The sound of two pairs of boots came closer. They were not French boots, but German. They passed my hiding place. For a split second I could see them. Two colossal German MP's: they kept their flashlights straight ahead of them, not left, not right, not into my doorway. I held my breath. They passed me . . . they were gone. I stayed there another ten to twelve minutes until there was no noise anymore and I continued my walk to the Station, where I arrived shortly before 11 o'clock.

The trains were slow in those days. Two policemen boarded ours. They looked attentively at my permit and at my identity card, glanced at me and went on to the next passenger. Frenchmen who were always quick to start a conversation were taciturn now. The three people in my compartment tried to sleep. I never could sleep on the train, and this was a long night.

At 7 AM, I arrived in Florac and left my suitcase at the station. Everything was so familar: the platform, the station master's house, the little coffee house across the street. The station was deserted. I remembered the last time I saw my wife here on the day of my deportation to Gurs. Was the heaviness in the air or in my heart? I sat down on the bench and waited for about an hour. I could not disturb the Audrix's so early.

Where would I go from here? Into some attic or cellar to hide there with Sonia? For how long? Would we see the end of the War and taste victory? How much longer could we hold out. Sonia had been crying lately more than I had ever seen her cry. The years of the Russian Revolution, the long and dangerous flight into Bessarabia (which belonged to Rumania at that time) had certainly left their mark. Then we faced the flight from Berlin, the difficulties in France, and now more than three years of War with the continuous running, hiding and poverty. How much could we take? Maybe to join the underground maquis would be a good idea. A bullet in battle, after taking a few Germans with us, would end it all—and quickly.

By 8:15 I could not wait any longer and started to walk slowly towards Audrixe's villa. The sky was covered with running clouds, a light drizzle was falling. A few more steps. Here was the beautiful house. I rang the bell. I supposed they would lead me to Sonia's hiding place right away. There is Simone Audrix coming out of the house, recognizing me at the outer fence and rushing towards me through the narrow alley. I embraced her and she put up her most beautiful smile.

"Sonia is up already. She is waiting."

"Where?"

"Right here with us in the house."

The Audrixe's, these good people, had taken her three weeks ago from our apartment and had hidden her in the maid's room in their house, under lock and key whenever little Françoise (eight years old) was at home so she would not go in and discover her. Françoise's best friend was the daughter of a gendarme! Just what we needed.

Simone had arranged for her little girl to be with friends and out of the house all day. The innocence and ignorance of the child could have become very dangerous for the two of us. Now she had just left for school. Simone told me all this in the minute it took to lock the outer door and to reach the house. The house door opened. There was Sonia. I held her in my arms and did not let go. Then I kissed Mr. and Mrs. Audrix who had tears in their eyes.

Over good coffee and white bread we listened to Mr. Audrixe's plan for us. The Pastor André Gall, was actively organizing the hiding of Jews; he had talked to one of his Church members who lived near Florac and who was a school teacher in a small mountain village an hour's walk from Florac. The school house had on the upper floor two rooms, ideal for hiding, and Simone Serrière had agreed to hide the Jewish couple there. In general she went home on her bicycle after school at 4 PM, but today she would stay overnight in the School in Montmejean to receive us. At about 5 PM, Mrs. Gall, the Pastor's wife would pick us up and lead us to Montmejean, so that she could be back in Florac before it was getting dark. Mr. Audrix then sent somebody to the Railroad Station for my suitcase. We put a few things into our shoulder bags since we wouldn't need much up there in the mountains, and since we would have to travel light. Once out of Florac, we would be safe. There were two Police and Gestapo informers in Florac, a medical doctor, a miniature of a man, and my watchmaker. Everybody knew that and kept away from them. We heard after the War that they both were shot a few days after the liberation by the families who took revenge.

I had to tell the Audrixes, Sonia and Simone about my experience in Gurs and in Gignac, my dangerous traveling, the terrible curfew minutes in Nîmes and all those other frightful experiences of the last ten weeks.

"You told me, Madame Audrix, at my arrest two months ago, that this pen was not a gift, but that you expected me to return it to you personally. Here it is, and thanks to God."

I handed her pen to her, her eyes were full. Oh, that good and courageous Lucy Audrix.

13

A LITTLE BEFORE 5 o'clock, Mrs. Gall arrived with her baby in her arms. She had a bony face and a smile that lit up her eyes. A most interesting woman, a mother with four children at home and a baby in her arms. Those are the authentic heroes, not with guns in their hands, but gifted with a willpower, with a tremendous moral conviction and defiance of Evil. Annette Gall was one of those adversaries of evil nobody would try to antagonize. Of the same timber was her husband, the Minister, who we would meet later.

We kissed the Audrixes good-bye and left the house towards the unknown. Mrs. Gall and the two of us did not walk together. She walked fifty feet ahead of us, leading us through narrow alleys. After about ten minutes we were out of Florac, we had not met anybody. The mountain road began, and here she joined us. We talked, exchanged reminiscences of our lives and did not hide our anxieties and our hopes. They were simple and modest: to stay alive. To others it would be ridiculous to pray to stay alive; to stay alive seems a foregone conclusion which everybody takes for granted, so much so that people in general don't give it a thought. To us two and to millions like us, in those days, it was the greatest gift from Heaven, to stay alive, not to be deported and disposed of, to go through this fiery furnace and not to be burned.

The road led through a densely forested mountain and was climbing all the time. We had been walking on this winding road for over an hour when, in a clearing, a few houses became visible in the distance.

"This is Montmejean," Mrs. Gall said. "There are seven fires which means seven chimneys at work, seven inhabited houses, seven families."

"Somewhere there will be our new home," Sonia said. Again we walked through a wooded area and then, ten minutes later, here it was, on top of the hill which we had to climb. Some dogs were barking. They smelled foreign visitors.

There were old houses, built with rough stones and roofed with gray shingles. There were no streets but narrow crooked passage ways, hewn out of the rock. You had to watch every step not to fall. This hamlet was so small that they even did not have a church, just the school house with a huge bell. Two stair cases from the left and right, led up to a small platform and to the entrance door. Simone Serrière came rushing down the staircase to greet us.

She was a small young woman with a round, friendly face and a big smile. We got a hearty handshake and were asked to come in. Through a side door we had a glimpse of the large class room, but she took us upstairs to the two rooms, one occasionally occupied by herself. The other one would be for us. Though Annette Gall was in a hurry to get home before nightfall, Simone offered her a cup of coffee, then excused herself and left with her to guide her and the baby to the large forest path. We were alone for about twenty minutes; we looked around.

There was a fireplace in Simone's room. She had a table, chairs, a chest and a bed: hers was a furnished room. Ours was empty except for a large, simple iron bed. Our room had a window too, like hers. The old boards of the floor were squeaking in our room, but the bulb hanging down from the ceiling indicated that at least there was electricity. In the corner of the room I saw a big pail; this must be our toilet. We found a kind of narrow closet in the wall where we could hang our things and our coats.

We heard steps outside: Simone was back. Quickly she came up the stairs. Her large smile seemed to be a lovely fixture on her face. She busied herself around the fireplace where I now noticed a few pots.

"You must be hungry, Monsieur et Madame, after the long walk."

"Sonia and Jack, please," I interrupted.

"Alright. My name is Simone. Marcel, my husband and Tony, my little boy, let me go for tonight. They will do their own cooking: my mother will help them, I am sure."

"How old is your boy?" Sonia asked.

"Going to be eight, but is he a devil! I'll bring you a picture of him. You will forgive me. I did not prepare a real meal; there is not much around here, you know. We will have a lentil soup, an onion omelet and some sweet chestnuts, the specialty of this region."

"But that is marvelous. You should not have gone to all this trouble," Sonia said.

We sat down at the rustic table and in fifteen minutes the lentils were heated up—dinner was ready.

"First the important things," Simone said in her inimitable Southern accent, pronouncing all the word endings.

"During the day, that is from 8:30 to 4 PM, you cannot walk in your room because the floor is squeaking and that would tell the children downstairs that there is somebody upstairs. Except for the two hours from noon to 2 PM when the children go home for lunch. Then you are free to move around as much as you want to. After four in the afternoon, you are free in the two rooms, but keep away from the windows, so nobody can see you from the outside.

"You cannot open the window if it is closed after I leave nor close it when I left it open. The people down there, a very observant bunch, would notice it right away and would get suspicious. It goes without saying that you will not turn the lights on, after the villagers have seen me leave the school. I come every morning at about eight and I leave a little after 4 PM."

"What about getting some food and water?" Sonia asked.

"Ah yes, of course. I will always fill a few bottles at the village pump for you and bring them here, telling the people that I have some washing to do. Having expected you today, I have filled and brought up already ten bottles which you see here in the corner. As to the food, all I am able to get for you in the neighborhood villages will be sausage, eggs, potatoes, lentils and chestnuts. Soon there will be some fruit."

I looked at her in disbelief, because food promised to be plentiful, especially after my diet of the last two months.

"But this is splendid. Coming from Gurs and the Labor Camp of Gignac, I have not seen treasures like that in a long time," and I opened my wallet, taking out frs. 300.

"Non, non, Monsieur, eh, Jack, don't give me so much money, I wouldn't know what to do with it."

"Please take it. Marcel might find a good suggestion."

"You are too kind," she smiled, "but I really do not need the money, not right now anyway."

I insisted. Sonia had a nice hand embroidered handkerchief that she gave her, and Simone was enthusiastic about it. She probably had never seen such a beautiful thing. We talked and talked. At about ten we all felt that sleep would be the best thing after such a hectic and eventful day.

A short time later Simone came into our room.

"You will have plenty of time now. There is a book which my father, Pastor Baldy, bought as a young man many years ago. It might be the right book for you at the present time."

And it was. It was the Bible.

This treasure house is an inexhaustible source of meditation. While I read the Bible to Sonia, I began to understand that Simone was not just an ordinary woman but an angel sent to us to save us from the hands of the murderers. I felt that certain relationships, certain meetings of persons at a given moment hide a deeper and often secret meaning that you can understand with your heart, but for which words still have to be invented.

If you have this gift to grasp situations and relationships, you will enter a temple of understanding, at the door of which you have to leave your shoes of logic and ordinary reasoning—as Abraham Heschel says. For this kind of seeing things, certain qualities are required as intuition, humility, an involvement which knows no limits whatsoever; required are an opening up of your being, abandon and love at the highest level.

Montmejean was not a village, it was a dying hamlet consisting of something like forty houses of which only seven were still inhabited, with a few used as storage space for wood and grain and what have you. There was no telephone and no running water, but they had electricity.

After the five pupils—age six to twelve—left school, and after Simone left for home, a deep silence fell on us. Rarely did a human voice reach us; here and there was the barking of a dog. There was no radio. We were—in the real sense of the word—on our own in that ancient, empty room, and had no contact with the outer world, except for the sky above us. The great philosopher Immanuel Kant once said after a life of thought: the more I think about them, the more uncertain I become about things. There are—according to him—only two things that exist in reality: "the moral law in my heart and the sky above me."

We had a few books, the Bible, and a card game to play a solitaire. Simone had brought me a sketchbook, and I noted now a few ideas about illustrating the Bible which I hoped—some day—I would be able to complete. My Bible illustrations in later years had their roots and starting point in this Montmejean twilight zone. And so the days passed, and then the weeks. One day, Pastor André Gall came up with Mrs. Audrix to visit us. He told me the story of how our hiding in Montmejean came about.

Weeks ago Pastor Gall had asked Simone point blank the question if she had the strength to hide a Jewish couple in distress. She had thought for a few seconds, knowing the dangers her answer might entail for her and her whole family, and then she replied:

"I believe it is my Christian duty."

"This was an inspiration that came from far above into a pure Christian heart," Pastor Gall said. "No great theologian, no famous philosopher of religion could have said it better."

I agreed with him completely. Simone not only *had* her conviction, she acted upon it. She carried God in her heart and mind and thus was given a deep understanding of life and human needs.

Pastor Gall was a strict and strong man, a man so overpowered by "Christian Ethics" and their intellectual structure that in his fight for his faith, sometimes he seemed to overlook the small voice of the heart. According to what Simone told us, his sermons were vibrant and shook you to the depth of your soul. He would admonish his parishioners with the outcry of a Prophet: "Resist, resist with your blood the Evil that is upon us." In that only hour I ever met the man, I had no way of getting a clear picture of this remarkable personality. But somehow, while looking into his steel blue eyes, I thought of Pearl Buck's father, a missionary in China, about whom Pearl wrote a book, admiring his strength of character, his unbending principles, his at times uncompromising methods. But then she would have loved to see a little bit of the heart of her father which he certainly had, but which he kept in hiding. And maybe I did Pastor Gall wrong with my judgment—he had brought me two precious packages of cigarettes. He was the co-worker of Pastor Boegner who was the great Organizer for saving Jewish lives. Twenty-eight men, women and children in and around Florac were hidden, fed and owed their lives to him.

Psalm 5: "For Thou art not a God
That hath pleasure in wickedness.
Evil shall not sojourn with Thee.
The boasters shall not stand in Thy sight;
Thou hatest all workers of iniquity.
Thou destroyest them that speak falsehood:
The Lord abhorreth the man of blood and of deceit.
But as for me, in the abundance of
Thy Loving Kindness will I come into Thy House.
I will bow down towards
Thy Holy Temple in the fear of Thee."

Psalm 13: "How long, O Lord, wilt Thou
Forget me forever?
How long shall I take counsel in my soul,
Having sorrow in my heart by day?
How long shall mine enemy be exalted over me?
Behold Thou, and answer me,
O Lord, my God;
Lighten mine eyes, lest I sleep the sleep of death:
Lest mine enemy say: 'I have prevailed against
him;'
Lest mine adversaries rejoice
When I am moved.
But as for me, in Thy mercy do I trust;
My heart shall rejoice in Thy salvation."

14

In 1943, NOBODY believed in a German victory any more. They were getting ferocious seeing now that the War was lost. North Africa was back in the hands of the Allied Forces. The Red Army advanced towards Poland. Only against the Jews did Hitler seem to win. There were always massive deportations to somewhere not precisely spoken about. The Vichy Government was a caricature of a government. But even of the great Governments none intervened on our behalf or threatened the murderers with retaliation. Thank God for the good people who risked their own lives by saving ours, the Gall's, the Audrixe's, the Serrière's, the Lapierre's and thousands like them.

Pentecost vacations had started, Simone was on vacation at home in her little village La Salle Prunet (a suburb of Florac), the children did not come to school, and for the first time we could walk all day in the two upstairs rooms, though locked into the house. At first it was a little hard on our legs unaccustomed to walking; we needed some exercise too.

Simone had prepared fifteen bottles of water, that is a bottle and a half a day for drinking and washing. We would have to be very economical because every drop counted. Two big round farmer's breads, about 14 inches in diameter, were prepared, along with plenty of cooked vegetables, two sausages and hard boiled eggs. Some little mice kept us company, so we put most of our food supply in a briefcase and in bags, hanging them down from the ceiling. For nine days we would have to eat our food cold, since we were not allowed to make a fire in the fireplace.

As to our toilet facilities I had to bring the pail down in the dark, not before 11 PM as Simone had asked us. I emptied the pail through a trap door on the first floor into the cellar that had an opening without a door into the street. The cellar had no floor, just dirt and soil. For safety reasons, so as not to be detected, it was better not to empty the pail before 11 at night. So we always lay around in the dark, waiting for 11 o'clock. It is often hard to fall asleep, but did you ever force yourself not to fall asleep, night after night?

And then it happened. Everything blew up. We were discovered by the villagers. Montmejean was not a good hiding place any more because too many people knew about our presence. Here is what happened.

The third day after Simone had left, night had fallen quickly; the sky was dark without a moon. I was sleepy. Instead of waiting until 11 to get the toilet pail down and to empty it into the cellar, I did it a little earlier. This was my undoing. According to my watch it was 10:25. Slowly and noiselessly I closed the trap and went to bed.

We had breakfast the next morning when something terrible happened. All of a sudden there were noises and shouts around the school. Then the school bell was rung. I closed Simone's door to the staircase because through the keyhole I could see a little bit of what was going on outside without being seen. A huge ladder had been put against the wall, a man stood on top of it, screaming and raising a threatening fist against the window, that is, against us. Would they storm the school house? There was no doubt, our presence had been discovered by the villagers. Sonia was frightened by my pallor. What could we do? Nothing but wait. The school house had been locked by Simone. They could not get in, except through the trap in the cellar about which they did not then know. Then something happened that happens only in improbable movie stories. A key was turned in the house door, and Simone appeared accompanied by Mrs. Gall.

Simone, smiling, but very pale too, gave us the whole story. Early that morning she began to worry, dressed quickly and ran over to Pastor Gall.

"Something is the matter with our people in Montmejean; I feel it. I have to go there right away. Would you come with me, Annette?

"Of course," Annette answered.

And the two women got on their bicycles and pedaled up to Montmejean. Arriving there, they saw all the people out in the street, talking, gesticulating. When the people saw her and Mrs. Gall, they fell silent. But Mrs. Couret, the oldest in the village and their former school teacher, took Simone aside and told her:

"Simone, you won't leave this village today, until we know what's going on in the school house. If you hide a lover there, all right, that is your business, but we want to know. People say there is a ghost. Anyway some have threatened to go to the Police in Ispagnac, but I told them not to. Now what is it?"

"Madame Couret, you might as well know that I am hiding a couple, a husband and wife, good French people who don't want to go to Germany to work in their factories. They are fine people, and you will see them in a few minutes. But how did you find out?"

"Last night, R. Quet was near the entrance to the school cellar and suddenly he heard something like a trap being opened and something like garbage coming down. It could not have been a rat or a rabbit."

What good Mrs. Couret did not tell Simone, and what we learned later, was that the young man had been there in the cellar in the company of a young woman of Montmejean and that they were interrupted in their tender embrace in a brutal way, by some "punishment" from above.

Anyway Simone calmed the Montmejeaners and said that in a few minutes she would come out with us. Everybody should go home, and we would pay a visit to every house. They liked the idea.

Mrs. Gall tried to encourage us, telling us that nothing would happen and nobody in the village would give us away, but that she and her husband in the meantime would look around for another place. Sonia and I got dressed and were ready for our visits to the inhabitants of Montmejean. Simone introduced us to every family: the Laget couple and their two boys, all giants; to Mrs. Couret and her daughter; to Mr. Sabatier, his wife and their daughter; to Mr. Bouteille and his two daughters Marie and Yvonne; to old paralyzed Mrs. Quet and her son; and to the families that lived in the two houses a little further down the road. They were all very friendly and warm. We were conscious that we were making history in Montmejean's Local Story. In each house I had to take a welcoming drink. Since these drinks were all very strong and different, my walking after the fifth glass—a new exercise in itself —began to lack in steadiness. I explained that it was the crooked road, but they would not believe me. Not that Sonia and Simone had to carry me home to the school house, but I certainly needed a helping hand getting up the staircase in the school.

Simone had done the right thing not to tell them that we were Jews. Mr. Sabatier sometimes read the *Gringoire,* an anti-Semitic paper with Sturmer caricatures of Jews. For him we all must have had some hidden devilish horns like Michelangelo's Moses in Rome. He and his pals might just have been afraid to meet real living Hebrews. But good, authentic Frenchmen who refused the enemy their collaboration, that's a different story. Were we not all in the same boat? Somehow the bespectacled Parisian (that was me) and the pretty woman from Martinique (to explain Sonia's Russian accent we made her come from Martinique, a French colony) gave them an idea of the wide outside world, of the bourgeoisie and of the far off Paris they had never seen.

I sat down and wrote a card to Paulette and Boris. Since last November when the German troops had occupied Vichy France, the German soldiers and the Gestapo were all over this unfortunate country. Our repugnance to go back to Paris because the Germans were there was no longer valid. Furthermore the Jews in the North had learned earlier how to cope with the treacherous German and Paris Prefecture techniques used to entrap our people. There might be better hiding possibilities and greater protection by the population there, since Vichy and the French collaborators began to be hated in the North. Here in the South nobody had as yet any experience in dealing with them—except for the Protestant resistance that was just emerging. The population still seemed apathetic, and the Germans showed a low profile.

So I wrote to Boris, telling him that we lived in a most beautiful part of France, that I had frequent asthma attacks and had to stay inside (he knew that I had no asthma at all), where Sonia kept me company. He understood that we were in a kind of semi-hiding. It would be a marvelous idea, if he and Paulette would spend their vacation with us here in Florac. We had not seen each other for such a long time, and there would certainly be a lot to talk about. (Meaning: we needed your advice on where to go from here). I asked Simone whether she had any objections to my putting her Salle-Prunet address as sender. She had none.

When the two women left late that afternoon, we had mixed feelings about the school house as a hiding place. True, we were finally free to walk around as we pleased, we were not outcasts anymore, we could talk to people, look after ourselves for food and water; we could use the fireplace, could cook, and in the evenings we could read with electric light. All these were great advantages. But as a hiding place it had lost its effectiveness. We now depended on the discretion, the good will and the intelligence of people we had never seen before.

The next morning I walked down to the house door and opened it myself with the key Simone had left. We were not locked in any more. There on the steps was a little package. I opened it: two eggs and a piece of cheese. Now, how do you like that! A present from one of our neighbors and a very valuable one at that. It was not hard to find out that it had been old Mrs. Couret, the former school teacher.

We quickly made friends with everyone, helping them with chores which they appreciated very much. The Russians have a proverb: "Don't have a hundred rubles, but have a hundred friends." (In Russian rubles and friends rhyme though . . .)

Simone would be back in class in a few days. We bought a chicken in the village to prepare for the lunch meal when Simone comes back, to celebrate her return.

Mr. Sabatier looked at me incredulously when I asked him to kill the chicken for me. In his look there was something like a question: Are you really French? What Frenchman cannot kill a chicken? But in my life I had never killed an animal. I would not know how to go about it. So he twisted the neck of the poor animal for me, and Sonia prepared a delicious meal with a bajanas-soup (sweet chestnuts), good farmer's bread, potatoes and a bottle of wine.

Soon we would have the lentil and chestnut harvest. I naturally planned to work with my new friends and help bring the harvest in. This was the first time that I really lived among farmers. They were all very poor; after a lifetime of hard labor they did not have much. Mr. Laget, a tall skinny man of about forty with few teeth left, bent from overwork, told me one day:

"Life is very hard for us here. With care for the animals and harvest time on, we are often sixteen to eighteen hours on our feet. And if at the end of our 'course' (meaning: lifespan) we have accumulated frs. 30,000 ($2,000), we should be happy. That's why our children want to leave: it's too hard."

Simone told us that the two of us had very good press in Montmejean. Madame Couret insisted that we should give up all thought of leaving this village: nowhere would we be as well protected as here. If ever gendarmes or policemen would show up, Montmejean's dogs would start barking a long time before any outsider could reach Montmejean, and that would give these good people ample time to hide us whom everybody here called "Les Nostres", our own—in their ancient Provence dialect. All this sounded very good, no doubt, but we were worried, and for good reason.

Simone brought us the news from BBC that Hitler—after the invasion of North Africa by the Allies on the 8th of November 1942 —had ordered the arrest and deportation of Jews and enemies of the Third Reich from all of France, as well as Gaullists, Communists, and so on. The Allies were just across the Mediterranean, the French Fleet had scuttled itself, and Hitler was anxious to eliminate all potential supporters of a possible invasion of the French territory, but it did not look as if the Allies would come this summer.

I had read the Bible in my teens. I have never understood it as I understood it now. I do not mean the understanding, analyzing and interpreting of the Old Testament as thousands of Rabbis and other scholars have done through the centuries. What I mean is the complete submersion into the spirit in which these powerful writings were conceived. My understanding was a grasping of a revealed reality. It may be that the utter helplessness and the dangerous situation in which I found myself for years now gave me an inkling of what Jeremiah meant:

Jeremiah 30, 10: "Therefore fear you not, o Jacob
My servant, saith the Lord,
Neither be dismayed, o Israel;
For lo, I will save thee from afar,
And thy seed from the land of their captivity.
And Jacob shall again be quiet and at ease.
And none shall make him afraid".

In July the lentil harvest had come, and I worked every day with my new friends on the mountain. Sonia, who helped to bring lunch the other day, said that from a distance the hill looked so steep that she was afraid I would fall off. It was good to do some physical work after so many weeks of idleness and not even being allowed to walk.

Then one day, Simone brought an interzone card from Boris and Paulette. They would come with Maryse, their 13-year old daughter, to visit us and spend their vacation with us. They would be in Montmejean at the beginning of August and would "invite" us to come back to Paris with them. Would we go? How would we cross the Demarcation Line that still existed between North and South?

Not far from Montmejean, maybe a mile or so away, there was a small waterfall; it was about thirty feet high. We went there for a cold shower, since we had no bathroom whatsoever. Sonia in her bathing suit from Nice was happy and really in her element, coming from Odessa on the Black Sea. And we would have something to offer to the vacationers from Paris.

When Boris would arrive with his family, we would have long walks together and maybe a little fun for a change. He would bring us the latest news, and they were certainly much better informed in Paris than we could be here in Montmejean.

As to going with them back to Paris, I did not think it such a superb plan for us. But we would listen to their arguments and decide.

Then one day, Marcel—Simone's husband—came up with his son Tony, a charming little fellow of eight years. All the time I felt very sad and worried, even responsible—in a way—for the danger in which this little boy, his father and mother found themselves because of us. If, God forbid, we were caught, all three of them would be deported with us. Such was the German and the Vichy "Law."

When the long summer vacations were about to start, Simone promised us that she would come often from her home village to see if everything was alright with us. Without telephones we really felt completely cut off from the world. We prayed that we may stay in good health, because the smallest malaise or health problem would be a catastrophe under the circumstances.

These good people in Montmejean were farmers, hard working men and women. They really earned their bread the hard way. There was an outward simplicity in them, though family relations between parents and children might have been as complex as anywhere else. What I found out was that they were all obsessed with sex. Living close to nature and animals, life for them boiled down to rudimentary things. Most conversations, even beginning with the weather, came down quickly to certain gestures, unequivocal smiles, even explicit words and revelations. In Rome do as the Romans do and in Montmejean as the Montmejeaners.

Soon, three months of our stay in Montmejean came to an end. So far, so good.

Marcel Serrière told me that the German resistance to the Russian counteroffensive in and around Stalingrad had completely ceased months ago, that the whole German army and its Generals, among them Paulus, had surrendered. Furthermore, according to BBC, the Germans on the African front had given up Tunisia in May. A great Soviet offensive had started around Kursk and Orel, the Germans had no more reserves to throw into the field. The British Air Force was bombing German cities and industrial centers with the most devastating accuracy and effect day and night which greatly curtailed German armament production. The British lately were bombing railroad centers in France, too, now essential for German military transport and communication. The Germans knew now that they were beaten and that their "Thousand Year Empire" dream was but a pitiful joke.

Was this the reason why they were perfecting their murder machine in such a diabolic way. If we are lost, we are lost, they seemed to say, but the Jews go first. Here are some of the tricks they used: They would pick up people that did not look too French, on the street, and show them a piece of paper with ten numbers which the man—suspected to be a Jew—had to add quickly in a loud voice. It is a strange thing: though you may speak a foreign language perfectly well, you count always in your mother tongue. This is how they often got a Russian, German, a Polish or Rumanian Jew. Or they took a suspect to the Precinct and gave him the "pants-down" treatment to see if the man was circumcised.

In Gignac I was told by one who had escaped from Paris the following hair raising story. The Center where they assembled the Jews near Paris was Drancy. A man from the Jewish quarter in Paris (the Pletzl) who had been arrested with his wife and little boy and brought to Drancy for deportation to the unknown, had been given the following choice: We need your cooperation in and around the Pletzl, the Germans said. Here is what you will do. You walk on one side of the street and two of our plainclothes policemen walk on the other side. We dont know who is a Jew—the bastards are all shaving their beards now—but you know. So you will indicate to us the Jew with a nod of the head after he has passed you, and we will cross the street to pick him up. It's easy. If you don't want to do it, you, your wife and boy will be shot tomorrow. It is your own choice: life or death for you and your loved ones. The man did it. Wouldn't everybody?

15

BORIS AND PAULETTE looked good and brought a bit of the air of the big city to this diminutive mountain hamlet. Maryse had been a child when I saw her three years ago, now she was becoming a little woman with a knowing smile. Paulette still had her pretty face, but she could lose twenty pounds, easily. They slept in Simone's room next to ours (Simone was on vacation now in her home village). There were no toilet facilities, rather toilet difficulties; but we tried to solve them with the help of Mrs. Couret. All the population of Montmejean was very taken with the "vacationers", the men with Paulette and Maryse, and the women with Boris. Boris really was a ladies' man.

Boris, Paulette and Maryse arrived in Montmejean early in August. How did they dross the demarcation line? Boris had false papers. Paulette and their girl are French, but Boris—though having lived in France for twenty years—had never been given French citizenship. According to his fake papers he was now a Moroccan or an Algerian; his identity card, military discharge and ration cards went under the name of Saadi Merdjan, a name that sounds smelly to French ears. He had become an Arab; he looked like one. In case he was arrested, brought to the station and given the "drop your pants" treatment, his circumcision would have been Moslem rather than Jewish.

As to their plan to take us back to Paris, Boris brought us false papers for Sonia and for me. We would be of Russian origin (to account for Sonia's Russian accent), but naturalized French citizens by the name of Michel and Maria Potapoff; I was a mechanic by profession. (I only hoped nobody would ever ask me to change a washer.) Boris could only get the identity and ration cards for us, not my military discharge; and even that for a lot of money. I repaid him right after the War.

According to Boris and his Paris friends, the Germans were defeated, and some of them openly said so. Wait until America came on to the European Continent. The Germans had started the War with a thousand airplanes; the French had two hundred. The Americans were building fifty thousand. Wait until they would be here. But how long could we still wait? Boris who is a dreamer and an optimist said that those Krauts might be able to hold out for six months, maybe ten, but not longer. Italy had been invaded by the Americans and the British. The invasion of France would follow; maybe this fall. The Germans had their hands full. BBC was talking about German peace feelers. They tried to offer the Allies a united front against Soviet Russia. Those idiots!

Boris was a jolly good fellow, gay by nature with a large laugh. As a friend you could rely on him. But he was imprudent in money matters and, worse, did not think that a married man had to take his marriage vows literally.

This seemed like the ideal vacation for him, to be out in the woods and taking long walks, discovering the country side, climbing mountains and looking into new faces, preferably female.

Once we went together on a food gathering outing. I had never seen where the black market was, but I should soon see one close up. Simone had given us the address, the name and directions to a hamlet where we could get something from an old woman, Scholastique, who did her farming with a spinster daughter. We went to see them.

An ageless woman, maybe 55, maybe 65, dressed in a long black dress on which I counted four patches, Scholastique sized us up in a few seconds, and on her face there was satisfaction as if she said to herself: they don't look like Germans or like policemen. But when we asked her about potatoes, ham, sausages and other splendors . . .

"Oh no, Monsieur, not a thing have I; the potatoes are all gone."

"But Madame Serrière told us," I tried. . . .

"Ah yes, good Simone. Well, if you are good friends of Simone's, I may show you what I have left."

And she took us into her cellar. The whole floor was one mass of potatoes, at least one and a half feet high, and the white sprouts, half a foot tall, rose from all of them—an indication of how long these tons of potatoes had been there. So we put twenty pounds into our bags and paid for them. Boris, who had a little grocery store himself in Paris, had a sharp eye and nose for food. He took a ham from the hook, a beauty of a piece, smelled it, touched it . . .

"How much?"

"Oh, this is the last one left. It is for the two of us. We have to eat too, haven't we?" She smiled shrewdly.

"I guess so," Boris said, "I would not think of depriving you. But you better eat it soon, it begins to smell." He put it back on the hook.

"To smell?" She was almost furious. "What do you mean? That's unfair to my ham."

We went to the door. Boris nonchalantly said:

"Of course, we don't want to deprive you." Then he turned around: "How much?"

"It is worth much more as you well know, but I would let it go for frs. 200, since you are friends of Simone's."

"What?" Boris screamed, "did you say two hundred frs?" He laughed, turned to me and said: "Let's go, Yasha."

We were outside the house when Scholastique—knowing that she had made a mistake—tried again:

"Listen, I would let it go for frs. 175 because you are such nice young guys."

"Come on, Yasha," Boris insisted. I became a tool in the game, but I didn't mind. Her flattery had not worked. She accompanied us down the narrow path from the house to the gate.

"So, how much is it worth to you, tell me," she asked in despair. Boris turned around:

"A hundred francs."

As if hit in the face, Scholastique fell back, covering her mouth with her hand.

"Sacré nom de Dieu, a hundred francs for such a beauty . . ."

"And I would overpay, if I give you a full hundred francs. It may be worth frs. 75." He knew he had her in his fist. He smiled:

"I offer you a hundred because you are a friend of Simone's." Now he played on Simone. Poor Simone's friendship became a worthwhile asset in these horse trading techniques.

"A hundred and sixty," Scholastique almost cried.

"Come on, Yasha, it's getting late." And we left. Slowly. "Don't turn around," he whispered to me in Russian. After about twenty fateful steps came a voice from behind:

"Eh, you two."

Boris turned his head around but still walking away from the house:

"Yes?"

"Can't we talk? Come back here."

We did. Boris enjoyed it thoroughly. I thought we had played enough with her.

"Let's give her 150 and take the treasure home," I suggested. Not so Boris. He got the ham for frs. 110 and enjoyed every frs. 10 downward movement by Scholastique. She was disgusted and speechless:

"You are not really men, you are lawyers." (Vous êtes des avocats).

"Naturally we were discussing almost every day the plan to go back to Paris. Passing the Demarcation Line would not present a great problem now with those fake identity papers which were very well done. By the way, these papers were not inventions, but duplicates of existing papers of real ex-Russians who lived somewhere in France or North Africa. But where would we hide in or near Paris? Boris had a clear answer to that, too: In the house of Paulette's mother near Enghien (a Paris suburb), where they themselves had taken residence after leaving their own apartment in Boulogne. All this was very tempting, and every day we came closer to making up our minds. After all, this wilderness here was not an ideal hiding place any more. Suppose one of the good Montmejeaners told one of his or her best friends at Church in Ispagnac after Sunday Mass that there were people hidden away in Montmejean. Even if they beg their friends: "Please don't tell anybody," this interesting news would get around quickly and reach ears it was not meant to reach. Furthermore, Paulette argued that a winter in this rugged, backward country with intense cold and under those really most uncomfortable conditions for city dwellers as we both were, would not only not be recommendable, but outright dangerous for our health.

We really did not know what to do. Sonia was leaning towards the Paris solution. Simone did not want to influence us. If she said Paris, we might think the responsibility was getting too heavy on her shoulders. She insisted that there was no danger whatsoever for us to stay in Montmejean as long as was necessary, i.e. as long as the War was on. They all liked us here and would help us in every way they could. What I did not tell her was that our money was running out and that I did not want to be fed by her or our Florac friends. Boris had brought us a loan from Jeanne of frs. 2000—I did not know how to decide. If anything happened to us in Paris, for the rest of our lives—which could then be much shortened—we would only have ourselves to blame.

And then, an extraordinary thing happened to make the decision for us, a thing absolutely unbelievable even today.

One day, in Simone's room, Sonia was ironing, while I was reading to her—which she liked very much. She was facing the window, and what a splendid view it was, with the whole panorama in front of her, the beautiful wooded mountains, getting bluer in the distance. There was an open piece of road, right across from Montmejean, on the crest of the mountain, where no trees and bushes grew, about fifty feet wide, the only piece of the road where you could see people approach the village, before they would be hidden again by the trees. It was a beautiful morning, a bit on the warm side, the sky almost dark blue, a typical Southern sky, and if your brain did not always ask torturing questions and remind you of the catastrophic condition we were in, this would be an hour to enjoy and to be perfectly happy. Paulette and Maryse had gone for a walk.

"Where is Boris?" I asked.

"I think he helps Marie Bouteille peel potatoes," Sonia guessed, and we had a good laugh. Marie, about eighteen years old, was a pretty girl.

I took up my book again, and Sonia had her eyes on the ironing board. Suddenly and without apparent reason, she put the iron down, straightened up and called me:

"Look over there, at the clearing in the road. Is that not a policeman?"

I jumped up and looked. There were two policemen approaching Montmejean. We left the iron and the book right there and ran out of the school house. Bouteille's house was a few steps away. We told Boris what we had seen, and the three of us began to run towards the other end of Montmejean, for about half a mile on the so-called road which was not much more than a large passageway with two wheel furrows. We were enveloped by the forest and nobody could see us there. Then we let ourselves down the side of a steep hill, holding Sonia's hand so she would not fall. At the bottom of the hill, about 150 feet high, we settled down, covered ourselves with leaves and branches to be almost completely hidden from indiscreet eyes and lay there. It was 10:45 AM on my watch.

"You see now how safe you are in Montmejean," Boris said. "The dogs did not even bother to bark, as they had promised to. No, you should come with us to Paris."

"I guess you are right, Boris," I whispered. Sonia was silent. I knew she agreed.

"What attracted your attention, Sonia?" Boris asked.

"I dont know," she said. "I was ironing, and it was almost as if someone told me to put the iron aside and look straight ahead towards the clearing in the road."

"And then you saw the gendarmes?" Boris asked.

"No; first I saw one coming out of the tree covered road and then I turned to Yasha and asked him if I was seeing straight—there was a gendarme approaching Montmejean. He said, 'There are two,' and we began to run."

"Now," Boris became very serious, "who took the iron out of your hand and made you look over to the clearing at the very moment when the two policemen were visible for five seconds, before being again covered by the trees and the bushes?"

"I know who," I came in.

"Who?"

"An invisible angel who was there."

There was a long silence, then Boris the agnostic said:

"Maybe you are right; anyway, it's a miracle that saved us."

"They would only have been too glad to arrest three foreigners," Sonia said, "bring us to Florac where we are too well known to the gendarmerie already, and show their Captain how good they really are."

After about an hour and a half, I ventured up the road from where one could see the bare mountain top on the way to Ispagnac. And there they were: two miniature gendarmes who had been a threat to our lives a short while ago. I called Sonia and Boris; they confirmed that they saw two gendarmes about a mile away from Montmejean walking in the direction of Ispagnac.

We took the leaves and branches off our clothes and slowly returned to Montmejean, quite shaken up and hungry. Before the schoolhouse a crowd of about ten people was gesticulating and discussing something. Then one saw us approach:

"Les Nostres."

Everybody was happy. Paulette and Maryse were relieved.

"They were nice people, these two gendarmes," Sabatier said. "All they wanted was some food. So they asked whether there were any foreigners in Montmejean. We said, of course, 'No,' but they were nice guys, they meant no harm."

We three looked at each other and understood even better that Montmejean had outlived its usefulness for us. These good people could not grasp what a danger these two gendarmes constituted for us. They did not know that these two "good" Frenchmen had been turned into Jew-hunters for Darquier de Pellepoix, the Secretary General of the Jewish Affairs Commissariat, who had succeeded Xavier Vallat. Our people in Montmejean did not know and did not give it a thought that hundreds of thousands of our people in France, millions of us throughout Europe lived in constant fright and panic, day and night, many probably starved to death by now or killed otherwise. For these good people the two fellows were nice men, friendly, talkative, good Frenchmen as they themselves were, and after a drink—it was a hot day anyway—they left. Yes, a hot day it had been; and we Jews knew better.

When Simone, a few days later, came up to Montemejean to visit us and to see if everything was in order, we told her what had happened, and that even this small hamlet was a part of that vicious dragnet that Vichy and the Germans had thrown over the country. She was upset and did not know what to say. Anyway our mind was made up. At the end of August all five of us would return to Paris and try to survive there. She looked down, and a very stern and sad expression came over her usually smiling face:

"What has my country come to? I am ashamed of it."

So were we foreigners who had always loved France and what it stood for.

Before leaving at the end of the month, we would throw a party, we told Simone, to which we would invite the whole village and, of course, her and Marcel. The Galls would probably not attend such a party, otherwise they would be most welcome. We fixed the party date for August 23.

And what a party it was. We had a sheep killed. The women got busy preparing it, cooking vegetables and chestnut-bajanah; two bottles of Calvados (very strong brandy) were dug up. A record player and dance records were found. Then we got tables and benches and chairs together in the big classroom downstairs, and all the inhabitants of Montmejean showed up except Mrs. Quet who was paralyzed. But she got a wonderful meal and a glass of good wine. Altogether with Simone and Marcel we were thirty people, the whole village. We first had our good dinner—a fat big sheep feeds a lot of people. At 9 PM the dinner was over with quite a number of half empty bottles, and the dancing began everybody had waited for. I think there was not one woman I did not dance with that evening. The children, who always had entered this Hall of Knowledge with awe and apprehension, took a kind of revenge by singing loud and doing all kind of fooling around which would never have been allowed otherwise.

Then, a real piece of Breughel painting was acted out. I mean his famous kermess painting, where in the right foreground a middle-aged woman faces combatively and in dancing step a man who lifts up one knee and looks furiously at her. Mrs. Couret, the elderly former teacher, and old Mr. Bouteille, Marie's father, danced a Gigue, an old dance that had inspired many composers even before J. S. Bach. I had never seen a Gigue danced before. It was just beautiful in its rusticity and at the same time its unrehearsed gracefulness. We others stood around, clapping our hands to the rhythm, looking at their stamping feet, their movements and their happy faces. To be sure, Montmejean in its long history never had a party like this. Montmejean never had a party, period.

I felt the time had come for me to say a few words:

"My dear friends in Montmejean. Were it not for these strange and most difficult times, it is very probable that my wife and I, that Paulette, Boris and Maryse would never had come here and would never have known so many good, so many wonderful people. To be here with you gives me the strong feeling that France has only lost a battle and that the great humane and progressive principles on which French Civilization has been built, during the centuries, will come back in a short while when the Evil will have been utterly destroyed, never to raise its ugly head again.

"I want furthermore to address our dear Simone and Marcel. Heroes are rare in this world, but we have two authentic heroes here in our midst. It is hard enough to fight in a battle, when you have to. But through free decision and in response to your conscience to risk your life in order to save innocent people from murderers is the greatest heroism there is on this Earth. Let me thank you all from the bottom of my heart and in the name of my dear wife. As long as we live, a long time or a short while, we will never forget you. You live in our hearts. And now let's go on dancing and enjoying ourselves."

Simone was crying, so were Marcel, Madame Couret and Marie. But with the music coming up again, and Boris filling the glasses, we all were soon back to gaiety and dancing. We were dancing until around 1:30 in the morning, and then they began to leave. The next day we put things in order and cleaned up the mess. Mrs. Couret came—all smiles and happiness.

"Ah, quelle belle veillée." (Ah, what a beautiful party last night).

16

WE LEFT MONTMEJEAN on August 29th, spent the next night at Serrières' house in La Salle Prunet and hoped to be in Paris the next day, the first of September 1943.

We said goodbye to our Montmejean friends who all regretted to see *Les Nostres* go, and the five of us set out on a long walk through the mountain forests to Florac. Simone was waiting for us in her house. Of course we avoided Main Street with its Gendarmery (so well known to me) and took to the narrow outskirt alleys. After two and a half hours of brisk walking we arrived in La Salle Prunet, a hamlet (with no electricity) and disappeared in Simone's house. Mrs. Baldy, Simone's mother, a fine old lady, widow of Pastor Baldy, did not show us too much of her pleasure about the fact that the heroic venture of her daughter was coming to an end. Naturally, I took this feeling of a worried mother as a very normal thing.

Our plan was that Boris and I would risk the trip to cross over the demarcation line first and alone, without the women. They would follow us a week later, if everything went well with us.

The treatment or rather mistreatment of the Jews in France worsened drastically with the setbacks of the German armies, and it seemed synchronized with the German debacle in Russia, the quake in Italy now and their flight in North Africa. How far and almost idyllic appeared the peaceful days of 1940/41 in Langlade, when a humane Prefect was allowed to liberate me from a Labor Camp. We were now treated like wild animals that could be hunted down by anyone, Prefect, gendarmerie, militia, Doriot-gang, all those who had tied their fate to the Germans, and who themselves were now under pressure to do their master's will. In many cities, like Nice, there was a reward of frs. 5000 (about $330) on every Jewish head, male or female. The lowest instincts were lauded and rewarded. When I was in Gurs, a few months ago, I was told that 3000 criminals, pimps, burglars and thieves had been released from prison and made concentration camp guards. Some of our guards inside the camp looked like it. At the time I was arrested in Florac and sent to Gurs, there still had been a way out. If we were caught now, that would be the end.

(By the way, Dr. Maury, the Mayor of Florac, had been arrested shortly after I was and reappeared after the War, a broken man.)

There was such a thing as French Resistance beginning to form, but killing German soldiers did nobody any good and had the most tragic consequences: whole villages, men, women and children, were destroyed in retaliation (Oradour sur Glane was one). The story of Guernica during the Spanish Civil War was often repeated. However, this Resistance movement and the belief that De Gaulle, one of these days, would restore France and its blemished image strengthened those Frenchmen who—first timidly but now almost openly—came to our help. While the good French people had been afraid of the Germans and their Vichy acolytes until now, things were beginning to change. Now the Vichy fellows and the Pellepoix or Doriot bloodhounds seemed to be afraid and scared for their skins. And in their fear they were getting atrocious and wild.

Mr. and Mrs. Audrix came over to Simone to say goodbye to us and we held each other in our arms a long time: we knew that their best wishes and blessings went with us. Mr. Audrix brought my and Sonia's suitcases in his car, and after they left, we started packing. I made again a light shoulder bag, not to be encumbered by a suitcase, if I had to escape and to run. One never knew in those days.

Before we two left the next morning I told Sonia that I would write immediately on arrival in Paris, that she should receive my card within three or four days, and that she and Paulette (with Maryse) should be prepared to follow us in about a week's time. We embraced Simone and Marcel: our hearts and eyes were full. Before leaving I did one other thing. I wrote a postcard to Clare, the watchmaker in our apartment house in Florac, sending him very kind regards from Nice. Then I put this card into an envelope which I addressed to friends in Nice, asking them in a short note to mail this card from a Nice mailbox. Being an informer, Clare might show it to the gendarmerie.

We boarded an almost empty train in La Salle. In my rumpled trousers, beret on the ear, unshaven, shoulderbag on the side, I came very close to looking like a French farmhand. Sainte Cecile d'Andorre. How well I knew by now this railroad station. Boris and I had time for a cup of coffee. Then the other train came: we climbed up the four steps and we were on our way to Paris. The train was full; we had to stand in the narrow corridor that goes lengthwise through the whole train. The two entrances were at the two ends of the car: they had a certain importance in our plans. During the first hour of our trip we slowly moved towards one of the two entrances and stationed ourselves right near the door, where one car leads into the next through a little passageway. There we put our shoulder bags on the floor—making it our territory—and had a cigarette.

"The control of identity papers," Boris whispered, "comes in Vierzon, as you know. They are either German Military Police or French gendarmes. In any case, let them take me first because I have more papers to show them. You stay near the door. If they want to arrest me, you quickly open the door and jump. When we come to Vierzon, it will be night: darkness might be helpful. But you do as I tell you: jump. If everything goes smoothly with my control, then you will be alright, too."

We smoked cigarette upon cigarette. I thought about what Boris just told me. He is a great guy: he wants to take the brunt first in order to save me from possible arrest. How glad I am that he is not an "intellectual", and I thought of Mr. Sachs's advice: in dangerous moments, when you are in need of help, rely on a simple mind with a strong will to help, to be a friend, to get you out of that heat. Intellectuals seldom will do anything to help you. They don't have the guts.

We ate the sandwiches that Sonia had prepared for us and drank some coffee from our canteen. The coffee was cold; what did it matter. Boris remembered that Vierzon was about six hours away from Paris. Since we arrive in Paris at 6:30 AM, we should be approaching Vierzon by now. The control on his first trip was in the moving train, Boris remembers, not on the quay. What time is it? A little after midnight. We should be very close to Vierzon. We open a new pack of cigarettes. The train is slowing down. It stops. Maybe to pick up the controllers? Slowly the train continues. Nothing, no controllers. Then there are lights outside and the train comes to a full stop. We look out the window: VIERZON. So, they'll board the train now. Ten minutes, fifteen minutes, twenty minutes. The train starts moving again. We look at each other incredulously. Half an hour later, the train in full speed, I squeeze his hand firmly and long. Could it be that we were spared a control of our fake papers? At 2 o'clock we knew that the danger was over. There had been no control that night. We found two seats in a compartment and sat down for the next four hours.

Hello, good old Paris! The railroad station was full of people, hundreds of travellers, some porters, policemen and some shady onlookers. So, while we had spent our time in those backwood places and little villages, in camps and in hiding, running and trying to survive, life had gone on here in this metropolis almost as we knew it before our arrest on May, 18 1940. Almost. You had only to look into those faces and you knew, it was not the same. The deadly German air had blown through it.

"Don't think the trip is over," Boris cautioned, "there is still the tricky subway to come. Round-ups are pretty frequent in the Paris Metro."

We treated ourselves to a cup of hot coffee or whatever it was, ate something and went down to the Metro. I was surprised that around 7 o'clock in the morning the subway trains were filling up already, mostly with middle aged or elderly people. Many youngsters had been taken to Germany for work, many are in hiding to avoid it, and there are still a million war prisoners whom the Germans never sent home.

At the station Strasbourg-St. Denis we had to change trains. The subterranean corridors are endlessly long in the Paris Subway. When we entered one of them to get to the platform we needed, we saw at its end two plainclothes policemen planted there, unmistakably policemen, who looked intently into each face of those who approached them and had to pass. *Hear O Israel* (the ancient Jewish prayer) came to my lips. We were upon them; the meanest hoodlum faces in the world looked at us. We slowly walked up to them and made a left turn towards the platform, four feet away from them. Nothing happened. They did not stop us, they did not call us back, and we quickly disappeared in the crowd on the platform. The train arrived right away. We could still see that the two policemen had remained where they had been before and that they had not followed us.

"We will have a good drink, when we get home," Boris smiled.

"You bet, we need it." I was exhausted.

At the St. Lazare Station (my apartment was only half a block away) we took the train to Enghien; from there a local train and we got off at the third stop *Soisy-sous-Montmorency*. The trip was over. We were safe now. Ten minutes later Boris opened the door of Mrs. Mallet's house, and there she was. We embraced Paulette's mother, a small roundish sexagenarian with a constantly disapproving expression on her face. I knew from before the war, that she had never approved of or really accepted her son-in-law with his heavy foreign accent and his adventurous nature. Maybe there was even a residue of anti-Jewish feeling in this otherwise gentle woman, a feeling cultivated in France from medieval times on. She welcomed me to her house, asked us how the trip had been—all very matter of fact—and went to the kitchen to prepare an omelette for us. Could I tell her of our anguish, when in moments of danger our hearts almost stopped beating, of the approach to Vierzon, of the plainclothes men in the Subway, of the fright that is constantly in our bones? Why, she would not understand. "It was a nice trip," I said.

Boris poured us a *Trou Normand* (a Norman hole), the hottest I have ever drunk. That did us some good. And a second one: that did even better.

I needed some sleep after this last sleepless, terrible night; but before I lay down, I wrote a card to Sonia which Boris—with a few lines of his own—brought to the mailbox at the Station. I immediately fell asleep and slept like a rock.

Late in the afternoon—the days were long—Boris took me to the little wooden, garage-like house in the garden, where I would stay with Sonia the rest of the War, almost a year. The whole property was surrounded by a five feet high wooden fence: its two doors were always locked. Our little house had a larger room and a narrow (four feet wide) side room for storage or luggage, as well as a wardrobe for our clothes. A small chandelier hanging from the ceiling gave the room a touch of elegance, and—marvel of marvels —a piano in the corner. It was not a Steinway or a Pleyel, but one could play on it an honest Bach Prelude or Invention: I would be able to exercise again. How wonderful if we could get Sonia's violin from Jeanne. I called Jeanne that same evening. There was a long silence, after I told her who was calling, and then she repeated: "Jack? What Jack?" She did not believe her ears.

"Jack, Sonia's husband."

"Jack? Where are you?"

"I am here at the house of Boris's mother-in-law." I did not want to give any family names over the phone.

"Where is Sonia?"

"Sonia is fine. She will be here next week."

"How is Jacques?" I asked.

"He is fine. He's on a business trip." I know: playing shepherd near Lyon for more than a year.

"Jeanne, my dear, Boris wants to talk to you." Boris took the receiver. He told her that he had to be in Paris tomorrow and that he could meet his sister-in-law somewhere, and bring her over to meet me, if she wanted to. Of course, she wanted to. Boris asked her whether she still had the violin. Yes, and she would bring it and some music too. This will be the greatest surprise and the best present for Sonia when she arrives.

Maybe we did the right thing to give up Montmejean. Only God knows.

Next morning, September 1, Nicolai showed up to go with Boris to Paris. I almost did not recognize him. He looked like a very prosperous businessman now, had gained weight and was dressed according to the latest fashion. I had known Nicolai, a good friend of Boris's, before the War, and we had become friendly. He and his wife Ina had fled Russia after the Revolution and had come to Paris in 1929, via Charbin in Asia.

With no skills or knowledge whatsoever, he had sold cookies and cakes in open market places near Paris. Carrying his merchandise in a suitcase, he used to take the train every morning around six o'clock to get a good spot and table on the market. He made a modest living and had a happy and decent life with his wife. A few years before the War Nicolai had met a furrier from Poland who taught him the trade. Nicolai began to find customers, gave up his cake selling and went into business with the Pole. Boris had told me already in Montmejean that Nicolai had become a fervent collaborator with the Germans, had made a good number of franc millions by providing fur jackets to the German army, especially welcome to them in the harsh Russian winter. Boris had told me furthermore that Nicolai had taken a mistress of very unclear reputation, with all kinds of shady contacts with Police and gangsters, and that suddenly, recently, the Polish partner had been arrested and deported. When he had been a poor and decent young man, I had liked him and his wife quite well, though our cultural levels had nothing in common. Now however he had become a dangerous fellow. If I showed him how much I despised him for his dealings with the enemy, I would have an enemy on my hands who—thanks to his girl friend—could do me much harm.

We embraced. He had the same winning smile for me as always, but in his fast running eyes there was the question: "Does he know what I am doing or doesn't he?" I had to play the innocent and even to accept his invitation for dinner the next day. He had rented an impressive villa in a neighboring community, Boris had told me.

Lunel, Florac, Montmejean had their dangers for us; but here, all in a sudden, I felt danger from unsuspected quarters. Dangers from a man whose guilty conscience wanted to be excused and accepted by his former peers who—he knew—did not give a damn for his millions which were acquired with dirty hands. And simple fellow that he was, Nicolai wanted so much to be admired for his money. There was only one thing to do: to stay away from him and meet him and Ina just often or seldom enough not to arouse his suspicion of our utter contempt for him.

In the afternoon Jeanne came with Boris. What a joy it was to see this good friend again like a harbinger of better days to come; Boris carried Sonia's violin and a heavy briefcase full of our music. We talked and talked. After all there were three and a half years of events and happenings to catch up on. Jeanne wanted to know everything.

The next day I went with Boris over to Nicolai and Ina. She had not changed much—physically that is. But she tried now to behave and to move her body as she thought a lady should, and it was just pathetic. Before the war in our relationship with Nicolai and Ina I had done my best not to make them feel the enormous educational distance, the difference of status and origin that was obvious between us. We were all stateless, refugees, we all had the same priorities of physical survival in a hostile environment. Now suddenly, for Nicolai and Ina, in their not so innocent *innocence,* things seemed to be reversed. They were rich, and we had stayed poor. What else had any value in life? And Ina tried to play it up.

"Eat, Yasha, things like this you did not get in the South." She wanted to be hospitable. And really I had not seen such a table in a long time; a rich black market table with a heap of maybe two pounds of butter, cold cuts and fish, olives and herring, cheese and fruit—all this, while most of us were on the hunger line. I was disgusted. For them life had never been as good as from the moment the Germans had shown up.

I ate very little.

17

SONIA, PAULETTE AND little Maryse arrived on the 8th of September. When Sonia saw her violin, she almost cried. This box contained her memories of Russia, Rumania, Berlin, Paris, a life of studies and family love and — flight. Now we both would have sometimes a marvelous escape from a cruel and dangerous reality into a better world, the world of music, the world that Pablo Casals had called back for us in Montpellier.

Little by little we settled down; it was very good that we two had separate quarters. People show their differences more when they are living together. Boris left every morning for Paris where he managed a small candy factory for a Swiss man. He made a nice living. Furthermore, going to work every day gave him the illusion that life was *normal.*

When we went over to the great house for breakfast, there in a corner on the chest were the two cigarettes which Boris left every morning, knowing that I had neither a tobacco ration card, nor the money to buy cigarettes on the black market. Boris was a prince of a man. Speaking of him, I remember a small incident before the War that showed me the ethical volume of the man.

One day, after we had visited with them in Boulogne-sur-Seine, he said:

"Wait a second, I will take a pullover and walk you to the Subway; that way I get a bit of fresh air, too."

We walked and talked, when suddenly — he said:

"Let's quickly walk over to the other side of the street." We did. I asked him why. And he answered:

"Had we continued on the other side of the street, we would have met a man who has borrowed money from me some time ago, and has not paid it back yet. There is sickness in his family now. It would have been very unpleasant for him to meet me. So I wanted to spare him the embarrassment. I am sure he will pay the money back when he can."

This was the nobility of Boris.

Sonia was very ambitious. She wanted to study the famous unaccompanied Chaconne by J. S. Bach. This was contagious. I went back to my own old Bach piano album which had accompanied me from my teens in Berlin. The sheets were yellowing and falling apart. Besides the Inventions, the Italian Concerto, Fantasies, Preludes and Fugues, there was the Chromatic Fantasy and Fuga which my dear teacher Dr. Adolf Starck never trusted me with. It was the last and the most difficult in the book, and a whole page of the Fugue was missing, but the first part, the Chromatic Fantasy, was intact. If Sonia tackled the Chaconne which may take months of study I would take on the Chromatic Fantasy. Maybe my fingers were not yet that rusty. Together we again played the Handel and Schubert sonatas; some Mendelssohn. What a beauty. Were better days around the corner?

We practically did not leave our fenced in domain and garden. The news about the persecution and deportation of Jews that Boris brought from Paris was frightening. They were getting desperate, those Germans. The War was definitely lost for them. They were now being bombed by American and British planes in their own country, and they did not understand what was happening to them. They had always thought that bombs were only good to kill inferior people, not the Herrenrasse (master-race).

Hundreds of thousands of French young men went to Germany. There was nothing voluntary anymore. They were now forced into labor batallions and shipped over there. Many French went into hiding. Laval tried to, but could not prevent the deportation of Frenchmen. The Resistance was getting more active with some help from London. If they committed acts of sabotage, if they blew up railroads and bridges, I was all for it. But they should not kill German soldiers. For every German soldier (they executed) a hundred innocent hostages were killed.

The street where we lived in Soisy was a quiet, narrow suburb street, where retired French middleclass people had their private homes with small gardens around them. Each one was in the habit of minding his own business and trying not to peep into his neighbor's garden, an attitude which was very favorable for hiding people.

As to our financial situation, such a thing was practically nonexistent. Had we stayed on in Montmejean, with our frs. 4,000 left we could have made it for approximately six months. But here where Paulette and Boris bought often on the Black market, I could not keep up with those expenses. I told Boris that I would give him our frs. 4,000 for our upkeep—let us say for two months—and when the War will be over—may God grant us the joy to see it—I will pay him back capital and interest (meaning with a big present) from my earnings in monthly instalments. He said: keep your money. I insisted. So he returned frs. 1,000 to me for pocket money. I already owed him frs. 20,000 for the false papers, he had brought to Montmejean for us.

We never went out on the Street. There was no place for us to spend money in any case.

Badoglio had surrendered to the Allies in September. Italy was finished . . or liberated; it depended from which side you looked upon it. Poor Mussolini, a tragicomic figure, was in flight. So were the Germans from Russia. Let them know how it feels to be on the run, those bastards. I only knew they would not have to run very long, not three and a half years as we have done. The only thing I was afraid of was the thought that the world would quickly forget their crimes and take them with open arms into the family of *cultured* nations.

The summer had not brought us the American invasion of France which we had so ardently hoped for. Of course our lives depended directly on it. So we sat there and waited. There was a dim light on the horizon, some hope for the next year to bring us liberation from that nightmare.

According to the latest figures from London, the U.S. now had a hundred thousand planes. The once mighty Luftwaffe was helpless; one of the Allied objectives was its total destruction.

We sometimes played solitaire that Mr. Audrix had taught us. Boris taught me to play belote, a French card game. But I was really bad at it; something on my upper floor did not work well in that direction. However, the first page of the Chromatic Fantasy was taking shape. It was a very difficult undertaking. Sonia had the patience to work two hours a day on her violin. Music does miracles for our nerves.

Our relationship with Paulette was very friendly. Her mother kept some distance with those foreigners who had invaded her privacy, relatives of her son-in-law whom she never really could get used to; and I was sketching everybody who wanted to pose.

Madame Mallet had neighbors, a middle aged couple with a teenage son, good people, anti-Vichy. They would consider hiding a Jewish couple—for adequate payment that is—and we thought about our friends Simon and Rika who had to flee from their apartment, but who were not very happy in their hiding place. Boris would talk to them. Unless there were roundups again (which was improbable for Soisy), this seemed to be a very safe place indeed.

The days and evenings were endless. Sometimes we put on a record and listened to good music. We felt a letdown, an immense fatigue. Was it the counterpart of the greater safety of Soisy? As if we now could afford to let go a little bit. Or was it that we saw a great light coming up: our liberation and a safe life given back to us.

Simon and Rika, originally from Riga (Latvia) were now our neighbors. Simon was a specialist in Russian Art and an Art dealer. He had no inkling of Art History in general and would not know the difference between Masaccio and Botticelli. But he knew perfectly well a few dozen names of Russian artists and could distinguish their styles. He was a good merchant, knowing what to buy and what to sell, and when to do it. And he had an excellent reputation for his honesty. He must have had a lot of money. Rika was an engineer, had graduated after seven years of studying from the Polytechnicum in Riga; but in France she never had the right to work, and—I suspect—no inclination to do any, her husband making all the money necessary for a comfortable life. Rika was quite an attractive young woman, intelligent, but with a predilection for gossip. There was an incompatibility in character between the two, an unbridgeable abyss of education and knowledge, a great difference in their emotional disposition, even a bit of animosity against each other. But they stayed together.

Simon was scared to his bones. His own shadow became a policeman to him. Such a fright was frightening. For Boris he was good company, he played a good belote. At times they condescended to take me in as a third hand, and then I got it from both sides:

"Ballot" (French for halfwit).

"Dourak" (Russian for dumbbell).

"You better go and play on Chassenes" (in yiddish: go and play at a wedding—a very humiliating proposal).

"Yasha, didn't you understand that I asked for your ace of spade?"—No, I didn't.

It was getting quite cold, and we spent most of the days in the big house, because our "home" was unheatable. The thing now was to stay in good health.

Sometimes I remembered with nostalgia the bucolic atmosphere of Montmejean with its simplicity, the bleating sheep and their little bells, the long drawn out "boooh" of the shepherd. Here in Soisy we had the shorttempered city dwellers with their mutual insults and their crescendo altercations. Thank God, we could escape to our room, to Bach and Handel and Mendelssohn. The War and its strain had been going on for too long. Four long years. Not everybody had the ressources in him to combat stress and anxiety and fright for such a long time.

1944. January—February—March—April—May.—Five long endless months of fear, of events, of trampling on our nerves, of constant tension, of alternating hope and discouragement. Time went on, we knew, but time became meaningless. We lived through agonizing days and restless nights. Our great satisfaction was that the Allies now repaid the Germans a hundredfold and in kind for London and Coventry, for Leningrad and Warsaw, by salting German cities with five thousand tons of bombs on each flight with an Air Armada of fifteen hundred planes at a time—day and night. Armageddon had come to the Teutonic murderers. We were only human and we cried for revenge and punishment, so Justice could be restored in the World, where humans and Justice had been destroyed for so long.

And then, after a long lull, historic days were here. On the 6th of June, 1944, the great and so long hoped for invasion of France had come. We heard it the first time at 7:30 in the morning: The Allied Forces had landed at 5 AM between Cherbourg and Le Havre. Half dressed we ran over to the house to tell Paulette and Boris. We all embraced at these joyful news. The War was coming to an end—at least for us—the Allies would be beating the hell out of the Germans. We got dressed, had a bite and ran over to Simon and Rika.

"The Allies have landed," I screamed.

"When? Where?"

"Early this morning in Normandy with many thousands of ships."

"Yasha, don't repeat this BBC nonsense. Don't you see that all this is propaganda?"

Simon was always frightened.

"No, for once I don't."

"The Germans have built an Atlantic Wall which nobody can take."

"Don't say that, Simon. The Americans are here. Soon you and Rika will be free."

"It is very dangerous to repeat such senseless propaganda."

"Poor Simon," I said. "Is there no hope and no faith and no joy left in you anymore?"

"No, there isn't."

An hour later Nicolai—the collaborator showed up. Very pale.

"Did you listen to the BBC this morning?" Boris asked cautiously.

"Yes, I did," he smiled. "They are bad liars, those Englishmen. You don't believe that anybody can break the Atlantic Wall; or do you?"

"The Russians beat the hell out of them in Stalingrad. Why can't the Americans and the British land in Normandy?"

"No, they can't," his fist hit the table, his eyes were popping in anger. It was more prudent for Boris to stop this conversation with a collaborator who felt the soil crumble under his feet, but who—in his fright—could become dangerous.

18

FOR SIX WEEKS now the Allies were battling the Krauts, but did not advance much. If our trust in the American Forces were not unswerving, this kind of stalemate would concern us very much. But then finally on July 26 the U.S. armored columns broke through and German defense lines at St. Lô. The Americans and the British unleashed a tremendously powerful offensive, and the Germans were on the run, from France into Eastern direction, "homewards" as their song went that we heard one morning in Lunel.

It could not be long now. We were all excited and overjoyed. Even poor Simon accepted the American breakthrough as truth.

Sonia played her Chaconne now beautifully. To learn to play it by heart, took her two months. But now since she memorized it she could interpret it so much better and work on the tone. The technical difficulties were overcome. The same with my Chromatic Fantasy. I played the four pages by heart. It certainly would sound better on a better piano. Boris was impressed by what I was doing.

The little garden in front of our garden house contained all the subjects in flowers and trees to paint and to draw. Sometimes just a few leaves with their fine meanders in black and white, where I can detect a whole world of details and forms, of structure and harmony, in short: of life. The pencil is a marvelous invention, but you must first learn how to hold it and how to direct it. And it takes a long time. Leonardo, Holbein and Ingres are unequalled in insight and virtuosity, in love for their subject and power of expression when they take a pencil or a pen in their hands. Facing a piece of paper and projecting onto it some intricate and sublime life in the nature that surrounds us, I had a foretaste of all the opportunities which freedom and liberation would bring us, meaning: going back to Art and to my work with a better understanding and a deeper awareness of the power and beauty of life. All of a sudden I felt very strongly what the struggle against this Evil was all about. It was the battle of those who understand and love the beauty of Life and who worship their Creator, against those halfwits who destroy life and who ignore its Creator.

The Americans were breaking through in the direction of Paris. It was a matter of a few months, maybe even weeks, until finally we would breathe freely, and our lives would be safe again. I thought of all those American, Canadian, British and French soldiers who laid down their precious lives for us, and I cried for their mothers, their wives and children, that these young lives had to be taken and sacrified, so that the world could finally be free again.

The Germans, in full retreat now on every front, beaten and mauled everywhere, their cities demolished, their generals and Fuhrer in despair, did not forget one thing: they were still deporting and killing Jews up to the last minute. We who went through this period took a vow, never to forget these crimes. And if ever a day should come when those perpetrators of the most heinous crimes may be forgiven and the horrors committed by them forgotten, we would still be there to show our scars and numbers.

Paris had been liberated on the 24th of August 1944. The F.F.I., Forces Françaises de l'Intérieur (Interior French Forces) were allowed to be the first to come into Paris and to chase the enemy — sometimes from house to house. Those Germans played delaying tactics, but it did not help them much. Since we, that is Soisy, were straight North of Paris, we had to wait two more days to see the beaten and retreating German troops passing through Soisy. We could not help going out to the street and looking at their faces. They were sitting on their Volkswagens, cannons and trucks, pale, frightened and sick, machine guns turned against us civilians. Then they were gone.

I ran home, brought out of the cellar a mannequin, *Adolf,* which I had fabricated with an old suitcase as the body, clad into a khaki shirt, two sticks in a pair of old pants and a stocking head stuffed with old rags. I had painted his face on it which by now I knew by heart, placed a swastika on his arm, and we ran with this trophy to the Town Hall Square, where thousands of people had gathered.

We put up a gallows, hanged Hitler there and burned him. There was little exuberance, but many tears. We all were tired. We had suffered too much.

On August 31, Sonia and I walked all the fifteen miles to Paris because the bridges had been destroyed in the last battles, so no train could run yet. We went home to our little apartment on Rue St. Lazare, miraculously kept intact and with more than a fifty month old coat of dust upon everything.

We went down on our knees and we thanked God.

We stayed on in Paris three more years, to get our breath back from a four-year run, before asking for an immigration visa to the U.S.A. which we obtained in the summer of 1947.

Why did we leave Europe? It is difficult to answer this question. It was like living in a cemetery. Too many victims had disappeared. Not only human ones. So many values we had come to appreciate in France became casualties of the War. Spiritual holdings had diminished, delicate and noble feelings had been smashed in suffering and misery. Hatreds were alive. Physical and moral undernourishment were flagrant and obvious, nerves were brittle, revenge and killings had become a habit. Many of the old Vichy Fascists fought for their civil servant positions and thousands of them could stay on, keeping their reactionary and anti-Semitic attitudes alive in an ancient and very efficient Administration. Four years of poison leave their aftereffects for a long time, even when the poison is gone. Most of Europe had the ugly smell of a burned out battlefield with the dead ones still lying around. The smoke of the Gas ovens where six million Jews and millions of other nationals had been murdered, had not fully disappeared yet.

Maybe one of the greatest disappointments for us personally was that the French authorities did not keep their word given to us before the War, namely that if we volunteered for the French Army, automatically we would be naturalized right after the War.

Not only were we — after twelve years of residence in France — refused French citizenship, but working papers as well. Yes, they had the impertinence to write into my identity papers next to "profession:" Agricultural Worker, since that was what I had done under pressure in Lunel. I thought it was a joke. But no; the manager of the department to whom I complained, concurred with his employee that I from now on was an agricultural worker and that it would be possible for me in France to only find work as such. This and other little stories made us decide to run again and to leave Europe for good.

The memory of my ancestors who had lived for many generations in pogrom-ridden Russia, then the Hitlerian darkness in Germany, and its contagion even in France told me that Europe for us was no place to live. Europe was sick.

In October 1947, Sonia and I set foot on American soil and we have blessed God ever since for this privilege.

Not only was I allowed to work and to find my way in Art—which had been my greatest desire—but five years after our arrival we both became American citizens. Our Paris status as stateless underdogs in Europe, so depressing and dishonoring, came to an end, and we knew—while traveling—the blessings and the honor an American passport bestowed on you. I did not have to worry any more about the anti-Semitic and xenophobic rancor of a little employee at the Prefecture who wanted to make me a farm-hand, but I finally could work freely in the field I had chosen and was trained in, and I could develop my talent in this great country of ours.

My religious bent, nurtured and growing under the most tragic circumstances and in the anguish of personal experiences in cruel Europe, now led to a number of illustration works. Among others, *The Jewish Family Bible,* a commission I was honored with by the Consolidated Book Publishers in Chicago, religious educational filmstrips which I painted for the Board of Christian Education in Philadelphia. Furthermore the eighteen over-life-size *Prophets* of the Old Testament exhibited many times from Coast to Coast and many more Holocaust and non-religious subjects. I also worked for quite a number of years for NBC-TV doing court sketches, illustrating news programs and specials. The Yad Vashem Museum in Jerusalem acquired my sketchbook from the Gurs Concentration Camp.

We had remained in contact with all our dear friends in France and were in lively correspondence with most of them, especially with Simone Serrière and Mr. and Mrs. Audrix who died during during the sixties. Whenever we traveled to France we made it a point to visit them and to stay with each of them for a couple of days.

Sonia died in New York in November 1973.

Epilogue

I WENT WITH Natalie, my second wife, to Israel and to France in 1981. The dear cousins Paulette, Boris and Jacques had died. Jeanne was out of the country. But I could introduce Natalie to the two daughters of Mr. and Mrs. Audrix, Suzanne and Simone, to Simone and Marcel Serrièrre, as well as to their son Tony, now gray haired and in his forties; and to Eugene and Augustine Salles and their sons in Lunel. We even met old Mrs. Toureille, the widow of the Minister, in a beautiful Old Age Home in Anduze. It was the happiest reunion one could think of.

In Montmejean there were just two families left. The school house had been bought by an outsider as a summer house; in May they were not yet in Montmejean, and we could not get in. One of the rare old residents is the son of Mr. Sabatier. Little Jean was six years old in Simone's class. We did not see him, but did see his wife who was washing some lambswool at the same old village well where Simone had filled her bottles with drinking water for us about forty years ago. Mrs. Sabatier had heard a lot about Mr. and Mrs. Barosin, "Les Nostres", who had quite a place in the "archives" of Montmejean.

She invited her unexpected guests into her rustic kitchen for a good cup of coffee and a little drink. And this time I could walk straight in and out. There was nobody anymore "to make me afraid."